THE ARCHERS

The Official Companion

Radio Times (Incorporating World-Radio) November 2, 1951
Vol. 113 · No. 1460. Registered at the G.P.O. as a Newspaper

MIDLAND EDITION

SOUND AND TELEVISION
NOVEMBER 4—10

RADIO TIMES

JOURNAL OF THE BBC   PRICE THREEPENCE

At Home with the Archers

Left to right, Harry Oakes as Dan, Pamela Mant as daughter Christine, and Gwen Berryman as Doris Archer.
The daily life of this popular Midland farming family is broadcast in the Light Programme from Monday to Friday

THE PRIME MINISTER
at the Lord Mayor of London's
dinner in Guildhall on Friday evening

FESTIVAL OF REMEMBRANCE
in the Royal Albert Hall on Saturday
in sound and television

THE 1951 REITH LECTURES
Lord Radcliffe on Power and the State
First lecture on Sunday (Home Service)

A JOURNEY IN GREECE
Based on Laurence Gilliam's recent visit
Thursday in the Home Service

SIR JOHN BARBIROLLI
conducts the BBC Symphony Orchestra
in the Royal Albert Hall on Wednesday

CECIL TROUNCER
in 'The Guinea Pig' by Chetham-Strode
Wednesday in the Light Programme

ENGLAND v. NEW ZEALAND
Television at Saturday's Rugby International

BINNIE AND SONNIE HALE
in 'All Hale' on Wednesday

'ABU HASSAN'
Weber's comic opera on Friday

1951 BAYREUTH FESTIVAL—Recorded performances of 'Das Rheingold' and 'Die Walküre' on Tuesday and Friday
in the Third Programme

THE ARCHERS
The Official Companion

William Smethurst
Introduction by Jock Gallagher

Weidenfeld and Nicolson
London

To Peter, Diane, Marian, and Ronnie

First published in Great Britain by
George Weidenfeld and Nicolson Limited
91 Clapham High Street, London SW4 7TA

ISBN 0 297 78715 2

Designed by Helen Lewis
assisted by Martin Bristow

Filmset and printed and bound by Butler and Tanner,
London and Frome
Colour separations by Newsele Litho Ltd, Italy

The painting of Ambridge on the endpapers is a reproduction
of a Collector's Fine Bone China plate, 11 inches in diameter,
painted by John Stubbs and available from John Stubbs
Design Limited,
Park Lane, Fenton, Stoke-on-Trent, ST4 3JP (tel: 0782 – 336 332).

The map on page 36 is also reproduced by courtesy of
John Stubbs Design Limited.

Half title: Doris welcomes Carol Grey to Brookfield Farm.

Facing title page: November 1951. A front cover of *Radio
Times* highlighted the programme's amazing success.

Title page: Patrick Lichfield preparing to take Shula Archer's
wedding pictures at Hagley Hall, Worcestershire.

The publishers are grateful to the following for permission to use photographs:

BBC Pictorial Publicity, in particular staff photographers Prak Ash Maisuria
and Christopher Wedgbury at Pebble Mill; Members of Cast who generously donated
photographs from their own scrapbooks; the Birmingham Post and Mail
for several rare archive pictures; Heart of England Newspapers Limited
for the photo of Trevor Harrison on page 17;
the Express and Star, Wolverhampton (photographer Paul Turner) for the photo
on colour page 4 *below*, and for the two photographs on page 111.

CONTENTS

LOOKING AHEAD

Jock Gallagher

Recording in Studio 2, Pebble Mill, with the Archers audio supervisors Steve Portnoi (sitting) and Marc Decker, 1985.

There is a date in my diary that has been very firmly marked: 'KEEP FREE'. It is quite a long way ahead – 1 January 2001, to be precise. But it has nothing to do with any fantasies about enjoying a space odyssey in my retirement. It is, in fact, the day 'The Archers' will reach its fiftieth birthday ... and I am laying claim now to an invitation to join in the Golden Jubilee celebrations!

As the programme is on the eve of only its thirty-fifth anniversary, there may be those who feel I am being a trifle premature and perhaps giving hostage to fortune. Can what is already the world's longest-running serial really go on very much longer? Well I believe that the programme has never been better, and there is plenty of evidence that it is now strong enough to run and run (as my theatrical friends would say), right into the next century.

After all, what other programme can rival 'The Archers' credits – a duke and a princess in the cast, four mentions in the Honours Lists and a host of fans reputed to include Her Majesty the Queen, the Queen Mother, and the Princess of Wales? As Matthew Coady wrote in a 1984 *Daily Mirror* profile of the programme: 'If a soap opera could claim to be By Appointment, it is this everyday story of countryfolk.'

Important, of course, as the quality of listening might be, so too is the size of the audience – and there again we have every reason to be confident. Our latest audience research report shows the programme to be in very good health. The *Mail on Sunday* colour magazine *You* put it in a nutshell: 'The Archers is booming ... the audience is increasing for the first time since the 50s. From being a programme that nobody would admit to following it has become rather chic.' And with the new listeners has come a new and amazing interest in the programme. In the summer of 1985 the Three Counties Show remodelled its central leisure area as a permanent Ambridge; an Archers play went into the theatre for the first time since the 1950s; and a documentary film was being made about the programme. So many reporters and feature writers wanted to visit the studio that a 'rota system' was introduced for the first time in thirty years. On the commercial front a firm near Edinburgh was working flat out to make Ambridge model houses and farms; a china company in the Potteries was mar-

Casting the fourth Dan Archer – Ted Moult auditioned for the part, but eventually became retired Derbyshire farmer Bill Insley.

keting an Ambridge plate; and another Black Country firm was selling 'Eddie Grundy's Pork Scratchings'. There is also a range of 'Ambridge' wools in the shops, and an Ambridge knitting pattern book.

An astonishing revival has taken place, but lest we seem too self-confident and smug, let me confess that I have not always been so optimistic about the future.

When I first became responsible for the general management of the programme fifteen years ago, the writing was more on the wall than in the scripts. It seemed as if this particular soap opera was all washed up. After twenty years it was, not unnaturally, tired and weary. The writers had exploited almost every conceivable storyline and the plot was stretched thin. The actors were fighting a losing battle against an indifferent script. The audience – much more perceptive than they are usually given credit for and more influential than the professionals

care to admit – were voting with the OFF switch. The result was underwhelming: indifference was the order of the day. Indeed, the apathy was great enough to penetrate the innermost corridors of the Corporation and down came the message – which I received loud and clear (mainly because it was de-livered personally by the boss of bosses over an al-legedly casual lunch) – that unless there was a dramatic improvement within a few months, 'The Archers' would be rested. Permanently.

I could, at this point, become as inventive as any of the scriptwriters and reveal the heroic struggle for survival ... how I poached the editor of com-mercial television's chart-topping 'Coronation Street'; bought in new writers and pumped drama into the flagging plot. Well, we did do all these things and there was some useful reaction from lis-teners (half loved the new image, the other half hated it). But the truth is that what saved the pro-gramme on that and one or two other occasions was

... timidity: timidity on the part of managers like me, too nervous to make the final decision to stop the recording machine, switch off the red light and consign 'The Archers' to the history books. I, for one, did not have the courage to face the conse-quences of such an event because even at its lowest ebb, the programme still had a huge audience, so vociferous as to put any harridan to shame. I was terrified by the prospect of being labelled the man who caused the axing of 'The Archers'. It is quite difficult enough to bear the burden of being respon-sible for the death of Doris!

It was the reaction to that 'death' – 'Quietly at home, Glebe Cottage, Ambridge: October 26, 1980' – that convinced us that we had fully recovered from the paralysing apathy of earlier years. The news-paper headline writers restored our confidence and had a field day in the process. Unfortunately our plan to write out Doris from the script had leaked just before the actual event, and the Press screamed

Doris and her three Dans:
Gwen Berryman leaning over the fieldgate with Harry Oakes, pruning roses with Monte Crick, and on the porch of Glebe Cottage with Edgar Harrison.

eventually retire, we would not recast the part.

In February 1980, Gwen had a stroke – on her way home to Torquay after a recording session in Birmingham – and it was immediately evident that she was unlikely to rejoin the cast. She was seventy-five. However, personal concern for her far outweighed any professional considerations and, as we waited for the shock of her illness to ebb away, we did nothing but ease Doris quietly into the background in the storyline.

After several months, it became obvious that we could not go on with such a central character floating around in limbo. The writers were finding it more and more difficult to contrive plausible reasons for Doris's absence from the village scene. There was nothing else for it but to write her out permanently. She would have to die.

The scripts were written and the scenes including the death and the funeral service were recorded in secret. The service was conducted with the congregation at the Cherington Parish Church in Warwickshire, who were asked not to breathe a word to the Press. They did not, although they all knew the interest there would be in the event.

It was at this point that the story takes a twist which would be unbelievable if it had come from the pen of our scriptwriters. With all the recordings safely in the can, I went to see Gwen in Torquay to try to explain gently what we were doing ... and found her in remarkably good spirits, with her speech enormously improved. She immediately told me she was feeling very good and looking forward to getting back to work! Seeing her there, frail and still partially paralysed, I cannot say that I believed for a moment she would be coming back to work, but I didn't want to spoil her optimism and said nothing about the death of Doris Archer. In a hurried phone call to the studio, I asked that the death scene be postponed, and then rushed back to Birmingham. No sooner had I done so than I received several calls from Torquay, from Gwen's brother and the people at the nursing home where she was staying, that made it clear that I had seen her in a

in inch-and-a-half headlines. 'Doris dies tomorrow'; 'Doris meets her end'; 'Doris Archer to die shock', and 'It's Doris Archer's last episode'. There was hardly a newspaper in the country that did not carry the story. Indifference to the programme was suddenly a thing of the past.

The decision that Doris should die was, in a way, forced on us by a promise I made some years earlier to Gwen Berryman, the actress who had played the part since its creation in 1951. Gwen suffered from crippling arthritis and on several occasions came close to retiring because of the pain and difficulty she faced travelling to the studio. This sometimes made her very depressed and on one such occasion she told me the only reason she kept going was because she was frightened of what we would do with the part if she left. 'I should hate it if you made someone else Doris,' she said. 'There is so much of me in her that I couldn't bear it.' By way of reassurance, I promised her that if and when she did rare moment of well-being. The reality was gloomy. It would be best all round if we held to the original plan: the death scenes should go ahead.

Whoever else may have found it difficult to keep up with our changes of mind, our resident mole did not, and the Press was soon on the rampage. We could not deny the story, and listeners read all about it before we could let them hear it for themselves. This is always a very frustrating situation for the production team, who rightly feel that it can ruin things for the audience. It is, regrettably, something we have learned to live with over the years!

If we thought we were laying poor Doris to rest peacefully we were very much mistaken, for the story was to take yet another bizarre twist. 'Doris dies ... as union protests,' said one newspaper headline, and the *Daily Express* ran its front page lead under the banner: 'BBC's Black Farce'. The report went on: 'Just when everyone was ready for a good cry over the drama of Doris Archer's death on radio last night, a union turned it into black farce "You can't have the village church congregation singing the final hymn," said Equity, "you must use our members". Day-long crisis followed at the BBC's Birmingham studio. In the end, the three million listeners tuned into "The Archers" and heard the tear-jerking end without realising the script had been changed at the last minute.'

The change was that we had been obliged to drop the recording we had made at Cherington Church of the hymn, and substitute a gramophone record. Equity were within their rights to complain that we had not kept them informed, but that didn't stop them collecting a lot of stick ... including this piece on Radio 2's 'The News Huddlines':

Roy Hudd:
    Did you read all about the Hymns for the Archers recorded in a church in Warwickshire? Equity, the Actors' Union, wouldn't allow the programme to use amateur singing. Funny really, I mean, they've never objected to the acting, have they?

Rustic Singers:
    Eternal Archers strong to stay,
    Tho' days and Doris pass away
    Thy thirty years familiar fame
    Has come from staying just the same
    For thirty years we've sung for thee
    Recorded by the B.B.C.

Solo Voice:
    Hullo, is that the B.B.C.?
    Hullo, luv this is Equity.
    No amateurs please on the show,
    This isn't Songs of Praise you know.
    Slapped wrists for you, we did agree
    Pro's only on the B.B.C.
Church Choir:
    Oh Blast! We'll have to re-record
    With singers we cannot afford
    The lines we've said,
    The lines we've toed,
    To make this classic episode
    In which the man from Equity
    Pinched Doris's publicity.

The Times, too, decided to do a bit of thundering ... in an elegant and witty leader. But Equity's General Secretary, Peter Plouviez, put the whole thing into perspective with his reply to the famous Readers' Letters Page:

Sir, Because my newspapers are not delivered earlier, I first heard of your editorial 'A death in Ambridge' (October 29) on a BBC early morning news programme. The short quotation they gave indicated that you were making a serious, if not actually vicious attack on Equity. I quickly drafted a reply, dripping with outrage and containing an odd snide passage or two of comment on the peculiarly inopportune moment *The Times* had chosen to give advice on industrial relations.

When eventually I read the whole piece, I was delighted to see with what elegant wit you had debunked and deflated the whole nonsensical and, I believe, BBC-inspired stunt.

However, I deeply resent the allegation that my name is 'made up'. How such a suggestion can be made by a newspaper whose editor we are expected to believe is called Rees-Mogg is beyond me, but rest assured that you will hear more of this matter when, as we trade unionists are wont to say, my executive has met.

Yours faithfully
PETER PLOUVIEZ

The only postscript I would add to that is by way of assuring Mr Plouviez that 'the stunt' was far from being BBC-inspired. If anyone had come to us with such a far-fetched script, we would have sent him packing to commercial television!

Of course, it's not only from the unions that we get it in the neck. The Church seems to keep a careful eye on what's going on in Ambridge. The Bishop of Truro, Dr Graham Leonard (now Bishop of London), carpeted us when the local vicar decided to allow Christine Johnson to marry divorcee George Barford in his church. It was, said the Bishop, a breach of Church of England law ... ignoring the fact that a working party under the Bishop of Lichfield had actually recommended a relaxation of the rule. And for those who asked why a real-life bishop should get so angry about a fictitious incident in a radio soap opera, the *Daily Mail* supplied the answer in its leader column:

> Surely because he knows that Mr Adamson is far more influential than any real-life vicar – he has three million regular listeners.
>
> Besides, this everyday story of country folk is unusually influential, perhaps because it appeals to the fantasy of the rural England in which everyone including the real country-dwellers, would like to live.

A new Dan Archer joins the cast – Frank Middlemass, with Bob Arnold and Chriss Gittins, August 1983.

In 1983, when Peggy Archer showed some interest in spiritualism and the same Reverend Adamson failed to dissuade her from straying from the straight and narrow, the disapproval came from even further up the Anglican hierarchy. One wonders what His Grace would have made of the seven priests-in-training at Cambridge who set up a fan club for Caroline Bone (then barmaid at The Bull) and were pictured swigging pints of beer with their heroine?

However treacherous may be the area of religious affairs, it is undoubtedly the politicians who seem to have most to say about 'The Archers'. Over the years, we hardly ever seem to be out of trouble with one or another of them. Going back to the very early days, the programme was regarded as being so influential that members of the cast – much in demand for all kinds of personal appearances – were banned from opening fêtes for any of the political parties. It was realized that the Conservatives held more events than either of the other parties and 'The Archers' might have been thought to favour them.

Throughout the years since then, we have apparently been guilty of the worst offence in any politician's book – bias against *them* – on scores of occasions. The Left has clobbered us for everything from letting Shula Archer join the Young Conservatives to promoting blood sports; from espousing support for grammar schools to being pro-Common Market. The Right has hammered us for everything from publicizing CND to being sympathetic to trade unions; from questioning the sale of council houses to being critical of local government changes. Somehow the complaints always seem to arrive on Fleet Street desks and over the past two or three years, the headlines have made the programme ... 'An everyday story of Radical Folk'; 'An everyday story of CND Folk'; 'An everyday story of feminist folk'; and 'An everyday story of True Blue folk'.

In fact, no allegation has ever been found to be justified and it is worth noting that none of the complaints have ever been pursued beyond the publicity value.

Ready as they are to complain, the politicians are more eager to try to use the programme for their own ends. We had a plea from one prominent educationist to 'help remove the vast ignorance among the public about middle schools' and spread the word about their achievements. 'Why can't we have Ambridge Middle School?' he asked, obviously unconcerned by the fact (or is it fiction?) that the village population could not sustain such a school. Another activist wanted us to ignore the reality of country life and import a couple of black families into Ambridge. 'The villagers are all decent people and I'm sure they would welcome the newcomers in a way that could be an invaluable lesson in community relations,' he wrote. In fact, if we had put them into the story and allowed them to be treated the way many strangers are when they intrude into a tightly-knit community, the likelihood is that we would have been reported by that same man to the Race Relations Board!

Not all attempts at getting in on the act come from the politicians, and the programme's mailbag includes letters which are beautifully typed on expensive notepaper from expensive public relations companies trying to justify their high fees by peddling their clients' interests. The vast majority of these are dealt with swiftly, and polite, but negative, responses are made. Occasionally, however, the odd letter does ring bells. The public relations officer of a Norwich shoe manufacturer wrote complaining about an episode in which Pat Archer was heard buying a pair of shoes for her son without having his feet properly measured. Editor William Smethurst, with a young daughter of his own, recognized his shortcoming and, admitting guilt, replied: 'Now that you have brought it to my attention, I too am appalled at Pat's behaviour over buying shoes for John. I will bring your letter to the attention of our writers at our next script meeting.' He did ... and Pat has been a much more careful shopper ever since.

Our general listeners, at least those without axes to grind, are also a constant source of helpful information and advice. They keep us up to date on all manner of matters, from some small piece of country-lore handed down from granny to the latest technique in pig-breeding which we might not have caught up with in the technical journals. All this is meticulously fed into our reference system and a surprising amount eventually finds its way into the scripts. Indeed, I would claim that we are second only to Terry Wogan (in his Radio 2 days) in feeding off our listeners. Also like Terry, we get our fair share of insults, although sad to say not all our detractors are as tongue-in-cheek as his. I personally took one recent missive with difficulty:

Referring to my letter concerning the drop in standards of 'The Archers', I was about to send you a letter just before Christmas congratulating the welcome change from the gutter squalor we had over the years been forced to hear. The change to interesting farming matters, plenty of humour, and all held together with a strong family flavour came to all who had complained to me, as a welcome relief. That is till last Friday, and it seems that Mr Jock Gallagher just had to revert to the usual slut tactics again.... Now we have to hear that the barmaid is having illicit sex with the Archers' farm-hand, Neil, and to make sure everyone is aware of it, Gallagher makes everyone to date approve, which is absolutely against everything that Godfrey Baseley intended. I have had dozens and dozens of critical, heated, furious parents complaining that just as they knew the family could tune in once more to the Archers without the usual womanising, illicit, grovelling-in-the gutter sex activities, it has returned to the low standard

The Duke of Westminster recording at Pebble Mill with Sara Coward (Caroline) and Arnold Peters (Jack Woolley).

that these lazy script writers have reduced this really potentially excellent serial. . . .

The letter was, of course, signed 'Yours sincerely' and, although I found it hard to believe, it came from a master at a public school. Despite the highly emotive terms of the letter, it does highlight one issue that is often raised and does need answering. It is perhaps the easiest allegation to deal with, although it is the most serious one. . . . that we don't give enough thought to moral standards and don't care what the public think. In every programme-making area of the BBC, the balances and counter-balances of public taste and public opinion are under constant scrutiny; to a degree that we are sometimes accused of spending more time talking about programmes than making them. With 'The Archers' – conscious as we are of its now very special role – the scrutiny is even more rigorous and the history of the programme's script meetings is one of constant rows about the use of language, the stance to be taken on contemporary social issues, and just how much stark realism should be allowed into the story. No decision is reached lightly and, while we don't claim infallibility, we can honestly reject all charges of not caring.

Another common accusation is that there are fewer real farming stories in the programme – and that, too, is a charge I would refute. It is true that there is no longer any 'Ministry of Agriculture' propaganda (and that has been so for at least all of the fifteen years that I have been involved with the programme), but comparisons between early scripts and today's disprove claims that it has somehow drifted away from The Soil. A key member of the programme team is the Agricultural Adviser, Anthony Parkin (recently retired as the BBC's Agricultural Editor, Radio) and he makes it his business to ensure that there is a strong farming content and that it is accurate.

He does this by drawing up an annual calendar of farming routines, providing monthly notes and reading *every* script before it goes into production. The calendar allows the writers (who can be working more than two months ahead of broadcasting) to be up to date on everything from lambing to harvesting, and his checking of scripts prevents any

Agricultural Story Editor Anthony Parkin taking writers on a farm visit in April 1985.

blunders on the air. His monthly notes not only give detailed information but also suggest specific storylines. For example, it was this note from Anthony that led to the setting up of Jack Woolley's shooting syndicate:

Shooting is growing so expensive that more and more shoots are going out of private hands into the hands of rich syndicates. Even large landowners now let their shooting and reserve a set number of days shooting, on their own land, for themselves and their friends.

This means that they at least get the chance to see what sort of folk are renting their shooting, whether they are adequate shots or the sort of urban duffers who miss or wound more birds than they kill. . . .

One landowner I know regularly goes out with the beaters, to keep a private eye on his paying guests, but one of them took a shot at a too low bird and 'winged' his host last year.

This man does not let his shoot by the season but by the day to people who will pay £200 for the privilege of shooting pheasants. He has to say in advance approximately what he expects the bag to be, although he obviously cannot be held responsible if the standard of marksmanship is bad and they miss an unusual number of birds.

Regular listeners will be able to recognize just how much of that has been worked into the programme in recent years, during which Anthony Parkin has gone one stage further than being adviser. He has also become an occasional writer and now that he has retired from his editor's job, it is hoped he will be strengthening the programme's farming roots even further . . . by writing more often.

If he does, he will be joining one of the strongest writing teams the programme has had in its thirty-five years. Editor William Smethurst was originally a scriptwriter with the programme and his awareness of the special pressures of creating to order and to immovable deadlines has allowed him to find exactly the right combination of talents.

Today's writers are young – in their late twenties or early thirties for the most part – and most of them are women, which is actually more surprising than it might seem. Between 1951 and the mid-1970s, when Tessa Diamond was recruited by script editor Charles Lefeaux, there was not a single woman writer. Now, out of seven members of the regular team, there are no less than five!

One of the newest writers, Londoner Margaret Phelan, makes friends with a little lamb.

Joanna Toye joined the programme as a production secretary and is now a member of the writing team.

They are Helen Leadbeater, the longest-serving member of the team who also works as a solicitor's clerk in London; Debbie Cook, who wrote words and music for the hit song 'The Day We Went To Bangor'; Margaret Phelan, who is also a qualified midwife; Mary Cutler, a Birmingham schoolteacher; and Joanna Toye, a Cambridge graduate who joined William's office five years ago as a production secretary. The heavily outnumbered men on the team are agricultural journalist Graham Harvey and Gloucestershire writer Simon Frith.

To this hand-picked team William Smethurst acts as coach and conductor. As demanding as any First Division soccer boss he coaxes, cajoles, flatters and, where necessary, bullies the writers to produce better stories, better dialogue, better characterization. He sees the programme as a social comedy of English rural life and is determined that it should be *good* social comedy, and genuinely true to the countryside today. William is totally uninhibited by rules, regulations, and bureaucratic niceties, and his very positive style of leadership owes more to instinct than to the management textbook. The result is a creative tension that produces a constant flow of stories and scripts, fresh enough to go on holding the listeners' interest even after thirty-five years.

For most of the listeners, however, the writers are only shadowy figures referred to once a week in the closing credits of the programme. It is the actors and actresses who bring the personalities of Ambridge to life and, not unnaturally, it is they who get all the fan mail. Over the years writers have changed without anyone paying much notice, but let anything happen to any of the principal characters

Diane Culverhouse joined as a secretary in 1980 and was rapidly promoted to a key role in developing the programme. She has written four weeks' scripts, regularly directs in the studio, and is Producer of the 'Archers Roadshow'.

(or the actors who play them) and there is always swift reaction. A recent example was when Nigel Pargetter was written out of the script via a long trip to Zimbabwe! No sooner had he picked up his travellers' cheques than an appeal organization was set up by a listener in Dorset. Mrs Vicky Johnston soon had letters from all over the country pouring into William Smethurst's office.

One distraught girl wrote: 'I am getting married in three days, but even so I am finding time to write in support of not losing Nigel,' and she urged Mrs Johnston to do all she could 'to bring him home – where he needs to be to be happy and where we need him.'

Mrs Johnston's own view was that Nigel's departure 'was rather worse than Grace dying', which would perhaps explain why she put so much energy into the campaign: 'Please forgive haywire typing. It is about one a.m. in the morning, but I simply must answer all the letters.' Just in case the problem was that we couldn't think of a suitable storyline for Nigel, the protesters offered the suggestion.... 'perhaps he could return and open his own gorillagram/kissogram agency'. And to show that she had learned a thing or two from the striking miners, another woman wrote: 'Do you think pickets at the BBC would help?'

Luckily William Smethurst had already succumbed to the more gentle persuasion and young Nigel was sent a return ticket before a single placard could be raised in anger.

I suspect that it is the same tongue-in-cheek approach that has sustained The Eddie Grundy Fan Club for so long. Despite his notable lack of success either as a farmer or as a Country and Western singer, Eddie's fans have remained loyal and turn up at all the public appearances he makes at exhibitions and agricultural shows around the country. If the Press have anything to do with it, another of the younger characters is likely to have her own fan club shortly. Elizabeth Archer, at just seventeen, has been hailed in the *Daily Star* as: 'The Teenage Temptress of Ambridge' and likened to the 'Dynasty' sexpot, Alexis!

Even those of us who find *nothing* surprising about people's reactions to 'The Archers' were ever so slightly bemused when Eddie's wife, Clarrie, was named in the top ten of Radio 4's 'Today' programme poll for Woman of the Year, 1984! Now, we all knew Clarrie was very popular with the audience, but to convert the kind of cult following that the Grundys have into hard votes in a contest won by Mrs Thatcher takes some doing ... and defies explanation.

After that it was hardly surprising that there was an explosion of wrath when listeners thought that Heather Bell, the actress who played Clarrie, had been forced out of the programme. The newspapers reported that Heather had quit after a row with the editor, and that was enough to set off the letter writers. 'The programme continues to enjoy a revival and its rise in the popularity stakes amongst all ages over the last ten years owes much to the rich and colourful characters that have been so carefully nurtured,' began one listener from Derbyshire, who then went on to praise BBC Radio for its high standards. But just as I was beginning to feel smug,

Above: Eddie Grundy fan club stalwarts – disc jockeys John Peel and John Walters escape from Radio 1 to prepare a special cocktail in the Pargetter mouse-racing colours. Graham Seed (Nigel) takes a cautious sip, while Trevor Harrison (Eddie) sticks to his pint.

Below; Trevor at the Town and Country Festival, 1984, with one of the younger members of the Eddie Grundy fan club, Henrietta Smethurst.

there came a sting in the tail: 'Just who are the BBC employing these days, that major stars are driven to quit. If this is a sign of policies to be adopted ... or the expression of concern that senior executives have for the listening public, who are after all the customers ... I fear very much for its survival.'

The incident that sparked off the 'row', was one of those spats that occur in any tightly-knit group, where people tend to live in each other's pockets a little too much. It might have blown over in less-

pressurized circumstances, but the combination of press and public interest was too much and Heather left. I do not intend to rake over old coals, but it must be said, both in Heather's interests and the programme's, that the decision to leave was hers and hers alone.

Another example of the lengths to which some of the programme's more enthusiastic listeners will go to express their appreciation came when a group from 'The Archers' made a personal appearance at the 1984 Ideal Home Exhibition. To involve visitors at the BBC stand, William Smethurst had set up a series of recording sessions where members of the public were invited to take the part of one of the characters. There was no shortage of takers and one young man had travelled from Paris ... hoping to

The production team in 1985: Peter Windows (director), Ronnie Henry (production secretary), Diane Culverhouse (programme assistant), Marian McManus (production secretary), and William Smethurst.

play a scene with Shula Archer, whom he described as the 'delectable epitome of an English girl'.

This is not the only kind of appreciation the programme receives. To mark the thirtieth anniversary in 1981, the judges of the Sony Awards for Radio made a special presentation recognizing the outstanding contribution and the continuing high standard of professionalism of 'The Archers'. And we notched up another record when the fourth member of the team was named in the 1984 New Year's Honours List. Following in the footsteps of Tony

Right: straight from the Ritz, singer Hebe pictured with Jack May after her spectacular appearances in Nelson's wine bar, and her spot on 'Pebble Mill at One'.

Below: recording at Checkpoint Charlie, December 1984. The programme was broadcast to Germany and the United Kingdom from the British Forces Broadcasting Service studios in Berlin. William Smethurst, Graham Roberts (George Barford), Sara Coward (Caroline) and sound engineer Steve Portnoi.

A new breed of Archers writers learn about the countryside in 1983. Mary Cutler, Helen Leadbeater and James Robson were joined by Angela Rippon when she made a television documentary about daily serials. On the far left is Tony Parkin, and on the far right William Smethurst stands next to farmer Robert Wharton.

Shryane (the first producer), Norman Painting (Phil Archer) and Gwen Berryman (Doris), Chriss Gittins (who had played Walter Gabriel for more than thirty years) went to the Palace ... to receive his MBE from Her Majesty the Queen. It was on that occasion that we finally had it confirmed that Her Majesty was a regular listener. She told Chriss that it was one of her favourite programmes. We already knew – on the authority of Princess Anne – that the Queen Mother listened in whenever she could, and

another source had reported the Princess of Wales as a keen, if not regular, listener.

It was, perhaps, this degree of Royal favour that helped William Smethurst pull off what must surely be the ultimate coup for a soap opera ... casting the Queen's sister to play herself!

William had decided to include something about the NSPCC's centenary in 1984 in the storyline and made enquiries about a possible appearance in the programme by the Duke of Westminster, who was the chairman of the centenary appeal committee. The Duke accepted and, in the usual secretive way, arrangements were made for a special recording session. Somewhere along the way Princess Margaret heard about the plan – she is patron of the NSPCC – and when the Duke was at a dinner party with her, Her Royal Highness let it be known that she

The Archers team at Kensington Palace on 14 May 1984 for a top-secret recording of Princess Margaret's scene at Grey Gables. On the left is sound engineer Marc Decker, and on the right Steve Portnoi.

would quite like to make an appearance herself.

I must admit that when William told me, I thought he was joking, but when it became clear that both he and Princess Margaret were serious, hurried arrangements were made to record the unique scene at Kensington Palace. We would hardly have been able to keep it under wraps if she had come to one of the regular recordings at Pebble Mill. When we released the news, the Press had yet another field day and yards of headline served to underline the drama of the coup ... and that was emphasized further by the refusal of many listeners

to believe what they heard. Some of them were convinced we had used an actress to play the Princess ... and not all were amused at such assumed effrontery. I was glad we had the pictures to prove we had not cheated.

On the next occasion we wanted special pictures – those of Shula's long-awaited wedding – we decided to try our Royal luck again and offered the commission to the Queen's cousin, Patrick, Earl of Lichfield. Assuming you have not overlooked the front cover of this book, you will see that he accepted ... and added another chapter to 'The Archers' story by arranging a unique photo-session at the stately home of Viscount Cobham, Hagley Hall in Worcestershire.

The only trouble is ... what *do* we do for the fiftieth anniversary?

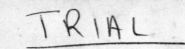

"T H E   A R C H E R S"

Episode I

Script by

EDWARD J. MASON   and   GEOFFREY WEBB.

Produced

by

GODFREY BASELEY.

Ø – 100

Cast:	Daniel Archer (the farmer)	Harry Oakes
	Doris Archer (his wife)	Nan Marriott Watson
	Philip Archer (younger son)	Norman Painting
	Christine Archer (daughter)	Pamela Mant.
	Jack Archer (elder son)	Denis Folwell
	Peggy Archer (his wife)	June Spencer
	Walter Gabriel (Dan's neighbour farmer)	Robert Mawdesley

1.   ANNOUNCER: Tonight Midland Region has pleasure in bringing

to the air its new farming family.......

THEME MUSIC

We present..... The Archers, of Wimberton Farm,

on the fringe of the village of Ambridge.

THEME MUSIC CONTINUES.

THEN FADES.

FADE IN ODD FARM NOISES.   COW MOOING (OFF MIKE!!)

FARM BACKGROUND.

2.   DAN.   Well Simon.   What d'you think?

3.   SIMON   Ah well - 'er might and 'er mightn't.

4.   DAN.   I know that - but what d'you think.

AN EVERYDAY STORY

Above: recording a scene in Hanbury Church, Worcestershire, Christmas 1951. Harry Oakes, Bob Arnold, Gwen Berryman and Harry Stubbs (who played the vicar) take notes from producer Tony Shryane.
Left: the first trial script, broadcast on Whit Monday 1950.

It was on Whit Monday, 1950, that some 50,000 listeners to the BBC Midlands Home Service heard an announcer say: 'Tonight Midland Region has pleasure in bringing to the air its new farming family,' and then, as the strains of 'Barwick Green' flooded in behind him: 'We present. ... The Archers, of Wimberton Farm, on the fringe of the village of Ambridge.'

The music faded, a heavily-pregnant cow mooed lustily, Dan Archer said: 'Well, Simon. What do you think?' and farm labourer Simon said the classic line: 'Ah well – 'er might and 'er mightn't' – and kept us in suspense about poor Daffodil for the next fifteen minutes.

'Wimberton' farm? That is not the only thing that sounds strange to modern ears. Dan and Doris were off, they told us, to market in 'Oldchester', and throughout the episode there was a kitchen-sink roughness to the dialogue. 'You know damned well I wouldn't leave her!' cried an indignant Simon (still concerned over the labouring Daffodil), and Jack Archer spoke in ugly tones about the 'blasted white fly' that were ruining his early tomatoes. Nowadays a 'damned' and a 'blasted' in one episode would guarantee twenty letters about declining standards by the next post.

But much of that first trial episode remains familiar. 'Well me old pal, me old beauties,' chortled Walter Gabriel, and there is a scene between Doris and her daughter – 'Twenty pounds for a holiday in Paris when we've just bought you a piano for your birthday? Oh Chris!' – that could easily feature the Jill and Elizabeth of today. There is some pretty harrowing emotional stuff, too, (apart from the agonies of Daffodil) that could be taking place between Pat and Tony in 1985:

Jack: I'm going out tonight.
Peggy: Oh, of course. Something vitally important to attend to at the local – darts is it tonight – or skittles?
Jack: Look – I can't help being me. If you don't like me you know what to do.
Peggy: Yes. I know what to do. And this time I'm going to do it!

And she did, too – leaving her little ones, Jennifer and Lilian, puzzled and distressed at Wimberton Farm, and heading back to her socialist, non-conformist family in London with a cry of: 'I'm leaving him. Jack and I are finished. We don't get on. And don't try to change my mind because this time I mean it!' (Theme music).

The idea for 'The Archers' had come two years previously, at a meeting between farming representatives and the BBC in Birmingham's Council Chamber. They were talking about ways to make farming information programmes popular, and a well-known Lincolnshire farmer, Henry Burtt of Dowsby, stood up and said the immortal words: 'What we need is a farming Dick Barton!'

'Everybody laughed,' Godfrey Baseley, the programme's first script editor, recalled later, 'including myself. But in the weeks that followed the idea kept turning up again and again in my mind. I began to think of the excitement that could develop from an agricultural story: the cow that lost her calf; the sugarbeet crop that failed; the importance of the February price review.

'Some months later I went to Lincolnshire and called on my farming friend. He mentioned his idea again. Pointing to a hundred acres of blackcurrants he said: "If I were to find blackbud rearing its ugly head among those acres of bushes, I would be as horrified as Dick Barton if he found himself in a pit full of crocodiles."'

Godfrey returned to Birmingham, made contact with the two 'Dick Barton' scripwriters Ted Mason

Intrepid producer Tony Shryane out and about recording sound effects.

The team that created 'The Archers' enjoying a day out in the country. Tony Shryane, Godfrey Baseley and script-writers Edward J. Mason and Geoffrey Webb.

and Geoffrey Webb, and secured approval for five trial episodes from the head of Midland Programmes, Denis Morris. If the above sentence gives the impression that it all happened over a weekend – well, it didn't. It took close on two years before Godfrey, with his two writers and sound-engineer Tony Shryane, were listening to the first episodes in the BBC's Broad Street studios, Birmingham. 'When the first notes of the now-famous signature tune came through the loudspeaker we all crossed our fingers,' says Tony. 'Would it be a success or would it not?' In London, the BBC programme chiefs also listened to the result (which had been recorded on huge acetate discs) and in due course the momentous decision was taken. 'The Archers' was to be given a trial three-months run on the Light Programme. The Powers of Broadcasting House managed to hide their undoubted excitement. 'There's no hurry about starting it,' said a memo to

Denis Morris, 'and before we commit ourselves finally, I should like to have a careful estimate of the cost.'

The agreement was, after haggling, a miserly £47 per episode. Godfrey Baseley was expected to incorporate the script editing into his normal job, and sound-engineer Tony Shryane was given the additional role of 'junior producer'. The only person employed on the programme full time was a clerk/typist who was paid six pounds a week. The members of the cast were paid between nine and twelve pounds a week, but to stop petty jealousy they were cunningly led to believe that they were all on the same money. This deviousness backfired after a few weeks when Norman Painting discovered he was getting two pounds a week less than Harry Oakes and threatened not to renew his contract. 'You stupid young fool,' Godfrey Baseley bellowed at him, 'You've got a job here for ten years if you want it!'

That, however, was in the Spring of 1951, when the listening figures were two million and growing rapidly. In December 1950 Ambridge and the Archer family were virtually unknown, and to help

Rehearsing in the Broad Street studios in November 1955. Tony Shryane gives notes. *Front*: Joy Davies (Mrs Fairbrother), Anne Cullen (Carol Grey), Lesley Saweard (Christine Archer), Gwen Berryman (Doris), Leslie Dunn (Paul Johnson). *Back*: Leslie Bowmar (Mr Fairbrother), Norman Painting (Phil), Harry Oakes (Dan), and Denis Folwell (Jack).

new listeners Godfrey produced a remarkable introductory programme – remarkable because it contained one of the 'secrets' (so long sought, so long puzzled over!) of 'The Archers' success.

He pretended that it was all real. Borchester and Brookfield ('Oldchester' and 'Wimberton' had fallen by the wayside), the fields and woods, the farms, the animals – and the people. He even went there, in a 'mobile recording vehicle' and talked to them. 'Mr Baseley's coming down here to put us on the wireless,' said Dan to the rustic Simon, and rustic Simon was not at all impressed. 'Gaffer, I've finished that bit of grinding,' he said. 'Shall I go up and stop that gap where the sheep got through?' 'Good idea, Simon,' said Dan heartily, and off Simon went. Godfrey Baseley was then taken into the house and Doris offered him a cup of tea, and Dan said: 'We're

rare ones for tea, here!' and after tea Godfrey went to see Walter Gabriel and said: 'We are going to come down here regularly to hear what's going on at Mr Archer's farm and put it over on the wireless,' and Walter wheezed and snorted and said: 'Wireless! I don't hold with these new-fangled nonsenses.' Then Godfrey chatted to Phil and Grace, and remarked: 'I've ... sort of ... bumped into a bit of romance, eh?' and Philip said, 'Oh no ... no ... not really,' and Grace said: 'Just friends.'

And Godfrey concluded his visit with the words: 'I found my way back to Brookfield Farm, chatted some more with Mrs Archer, made the final arrangements about the broadcast and ... well – you'll hear all about that for yourselves if you listen to the Light Programme at a quarter to twelve on Monday, the 1st of January. I do hope you enjoy eavesdropping on these countryfolk. Goodnight.'

It was amazing stuff, saying 'Come along, children, we're off to Sunnybank Farm' to the housewives and factory workers of grim, post-war Britain. But people didn't just enjoy eavesdropping on Ambridge life, they loved it. They were fascinated, enthralled, right from that first national episode which opened with Dan saying 'And a Happy New Year to all!' and Doris saying, quietly, 'A very happy New Year, Dan,' and Dan replying fondly, 'Thanks Mother. If it's as good as the last 'un I'll be satisfied,' and Jack Archer (oh, how his son takes after him!) piping up with, 'How about some more of that rich and ripe old cooking port, Dad?'

And so the story began, in that year of tea rationing and identity cards, the fall of the Attlee government, and the continuing drain of the Korean war. For fifteen minutes every day a delighted nation escaped to the world of Farmer Dan and his apple-cheeked wife, of their two lovable shire horses, Blossom and Boxer, their farm-labourer, Simon, and their cheery rogue of a neighbour Walter Gabriel. Of their family – Jack, the eldest, who had married pretty young ATS girl Peggy Perkins from Peckham and was having difficulties with his smallholding; Philip who was keen, impetuous, and in love with his boss's daughter, Grace; Christine, who had got her HSC with distinction in biology and a credit in chemistry . . .

Within weeks the audience was two million. By Easter it had been moved to the peak listening spot of 6.45 pm (killing-off 'Dick Barton – Special Agent') and a week after that the audience was doubled to four million, putting it in the BBC's 'super-league' with programmes like Wilfred Pickles's 'Have a Go', Billy Cotton's 'Band Show' and the amazing 'Adventures of PC49'. The BBC had a huge success on its hands, and the minutes show that Godfrey Baseley was advised to avoid indelicacies, and restrict the use of Americanisms where an English equivalent was available. In May, under the heading 'Not a flop!', the story of 'The Archers' featured in the hugely successful showbiz magazine *Radio Review* – next to an article about another rising star – 'the young bachelor comedian-impressionist, Peter Sellers.'

Godfrey Baseley, in whose fertile mind Ambridge first existed, had begun broadcasting as an actor and variety artist in 1929, and joined the BBC Midland Region staff in 1943. He became a producer of agricultural and gardening programmes, and when 'The Archers' became a dramatic success it was its farming accuracy that caused him most pride. 'Perhaps the most important thing in its favour is that it is authentic,' he wrote in May 1951, 'and behind us is

Norman Painting, Gwen Berryman, Lesley Saweard and Harry Oakes recording in 1955.

every rural organization of importance, ready to help in presenting a true picture of the countryside, and to bring a breath of fresh air every day to tired and weary townsfolk.' Tony Shryane, who had rapidly become full-time producer, was equally proud

Dan and Doris opening a fête in Norfolk. In the mid-1950s members of the cast were told to stop opening Conservative Association fêtes because of the implied political bias.

of his authentic sound effects. 'Recordings have been made at Women's Institute meetings, village churches, riding schools, parks and country estates, railway stations, farms, cattle markets and skittle alleys,' he was able to proclaim after a few short breathless months, and announced: 'The Archers employ an ornithologist who comes to the studio each month and listens to the various bird noises, so that we are always sure of hearing the right bird-songs at the right time of year.' (Oh that there had been an ornithologist on the books in 1984, when the Ambridge dawn chorus was broadcast in September!)

The writers, too, were caught up in this dramatic authenticity, this new 'wireless *verité*' that was being developed in Birmingham, and they found it far more difficult than 'Dick Barton'.

'When we wrote Dick Barton,' Geoffrey Webb recollected, 'I'd ring Mason and say I'm ending my twenty-episode story with Barton, Snowy and Jock flying back across the Atlantic from the Brazilian jungle. The engines of the plane have just caught fire. Will you carry on from there?

'With The Archers it's different. These are real people – not fabulous characters of the imagination. We might argue about what would happen if Philip

Editor Godfrey Baseley interviews a Midlands sheep farmer.

Archer found Bill Slater kissing Philip's girl-friend, Grace. Would Philip set about Bill? Would he turn on his heels and walk away disgustedly? Or would he merely say, "I wonder if I could have a word with you Grace, when you can speak again?"'

To help remember what stock was held on each farm (it was unforgivable, they found, for Dan to have 300 head of sheep one week and only 100 the next) each writer bought a toy farm, with model sheep and cows. 'But Mason has four children and I have two,' said Geoffrey ruefully, 'and we found the stock situation on the farms changing from day to day, depending on how many toy cows and sheep went to school in their pockets!'

At the end of 1951, with the programme holding six million listeners every night (a million more than Mrs Dale's Diary) Godfrey Baseley was able to look back, and declare firmly: 'During the year we set about big schemes such as the love affair between Christine and Basil Grove, and the ironstone story. But we find that what is really wanted is the straightforward story of the daily happenings in the countryside.'

It was not, however, what listeners were getting. The Ministry of Agriculture and the National Farmers Union might well have been on the advisory team, together with the famous ornithologist, the Y.M.C.A., and the British Sugar Beet Corporation; Tony Shryane's sound effects might well have been the most authentic in the world, and the writers scrupulously concerned over accuracy; but each night when the strains of 'Barwick Green' carried the nation down the road to Borchester, and along the sleepy lane to Ambridge, and up the dusty track to Brookfield Farm, it was actually in for a great deal of SEX and VIOLENCE and ADVENTURE.

'We have tried with success to keep 20 per cent of the material agricultural, 5 to 10 per cent horticultural, and a similar percentage country life and natural history' said an official memorandum – but what about the other sixty per cent?

Well, in the first year alone the slovenly Bill Slater was killed in a fight outside The Bull; people were hit over the head by saboteurs plotting to wreck an ironstone drilling site; Phil was knocked unconscious by a branch after leaping on the running-board of Grace's car (as she sped away, crazed with jealousy, after seeing him in the passionate embrace of willowy-blonde Jane Maxwell); Grace Fairbrother fell in love with neurotic, war-wounded victim of Korea Lt Carey; Christine was involved not only with Basil Grove (whoever he was!) but with *Borchester Echo* cub reporter Dick Raymond and mineralogist Keith Latimer – and in early 1952 she had a very strange friendship with a Lady Hyleberrow who hated her meeting boys and wanted to take her to Ethiopia. Also in 1952 Peggy Archer had to fend off the passionate advances of Jack's partner Barney Lee, and the Irish thriller-writer Mike Daly was exposed – not as the embezzler Major Smith of the Pay Corps, as listeners had been led to expect, but as secret-service agent Mike Daly MC, who had escaped from Dachau by being certified as dead by a pro-British German guard, had adopted the identity of embezzler Smith to throw enemy agents off the track, and had become the fiancé of Reggie Trentham's girlfriend Valerie Grayson for similar reasons of national security. (Valerie, a puzzled Reggie was told, was also a secret service agent. He accepted the various explanations and married her).

An everyday story of countryfolk? Well, that's what the programme-makers claimed it was, and perhaps the listeners believed it, as they tuned in to hear the slinky Baroness Czorva summon Mike Daly MC away on yet another secret mission, or a jet plane crash in Dan's five acre field. Predictably enough, though, it wasn't the outrageous adventure stories or the violence that finally alarmed the BBC (although there has been plenty of violence over the years, what with Tom Forrest killing poachers, Doris and Jack Woolley being left unconscious by robbers, kidnapping, arson, and cows falling on Dan from a great height) – it was sex that finally caused the trouble. 'The Archers used to be for family listening but recently it has become disgusting' claimed a letter that arrived on the producer's desk, not in 1985 (as so many similar have done) but in 1955; and another said about the goings-on of flighty Irish girl Rita Flynn: 'It's nothing but a lot of suggestiveness instead of a story of country life!' Much more alarming, from the producer's point of view, was a stern note from a senior BBC executive: 'I am getting a good many complaints about the sexiness of "The Archers" these days and I hear from my son in the Regular Army in Germany that it is now eagerly listened to in the Mess to see in

The *Borchester Echo* had several editions in the 1960s and early 1970s.

what shape sex will rear its ugly head each night.' Another sharp memo from authority accused the programme of having 'a cheap storyline and hardly any farming', and after a scene between Toby Stobeman and Carol Grey, yet another reprimand was received in Birmingham: 'It was faded out at a moment and after such scenes of heavy breathing and what you will, that could only lead one to suppose that Miss Grey had forgotten her mother's good advice – a supposition more than confirmed in the episode covering the following day, during which Miss Grey did a good deal more sighing of a retrospective and reflective character, and again left the more worldly listener in no doubt as to what had happened on the sofa . . .'

Whether shocked or worldly, fascinated by sex and violence or by the life-cycle of the warble fly and

DAN ARCHER

Harry Oakes

DORIS ARCHER

Gwen Berryman

PHILIP ARCHER

Norman Painting

JILL ARCHER

Patricia Greene

MR. FAIRBROTHER

Leslie Bowmar

MRS. FAIRBROTHER

Joy Davies

TOM FORREST

Bob Arnold

PRU HARRIS

Mary Dalley

JOHN TREGORRAN

Basil Jones

CAROL GREY

Ann Cullen

WALTER GABRIEL

Chris Gittins

MRS. PERKINS

Pauline Seville

JACK ARCHER

Denis Folwell

PEGGY ARCHER

Thelma Rogers

PAUL JOHNSON

Leslie Dunn

CHRISTINE JOHNSON

Lesley Saweard

NED LARKIN

Bill Payne

PRODUCER

Tony Shryane

Above: Harry Oakes has a fatherly chat with Pamela Mant during a break in rehearsals. In the background is Ysanne Churchman, soon to 'die' as Grace in the stables fire.

Left: The cast in the mid-1950s.

Dan and Doris singing 'Down the Vale', listeners continued to join the programme in ever increasing numbers, The *Daily Mail* award as 'most entertaining radio programme' was won jointly with 'Take It From Here' in 1954 and by 'The Archers' in its own right in 1955. In the summer of 1953 the programme was heard for the first time on the BBC General Overseas Service, and it was estimated that more than one in three of the adult population of Britain was listening. In 1955 the audience peaked at an incredible 20,000,000.

It was destined, worldwide, to find new listeners still, with sales to Canada, Australia, and New Zealand. But the seeds of eventual decline were already sown – and there was nothing that Denis Morris or Godfrey Baseley could do about it. Slowly but remorselessly television was extending its influence, and listeners were turning into viewers.

The BBC seemed happy to encourage the trend, and with some insensitivity asked if Dan could please lead the way by getting a television set. Godfrey Baseley bluntly refused on the grounds that every viewer gained for the BBC was a listener lost for him. In the end Dan did get a set, and Godfrey was proved right. But 'The Archers' did not surrender its pre-eminent position without a struggle. On 22 September 1955, Independent Television started up – and on that very same night, in a stables fire at Ambridge, Grace Archer died.

Accidentally or on purpose, publicity efforts for the infant television service were dealt a vicious blow. 'Listeners sob as Grace Archer dies' screamed the *Daily Sketch*, and the *Daily Express* demanded: 'Why do this to Grace Archer?' BBC switchboards were jammed, a doctor claimed the shock had damaged the nation's health, the matron of an Old Folks' Home complained that her charges were too upset to sleep, and the manager of a West Bromwich factory claimed the 'death' had held up production. Press interest went on and on: the *Daily Mirror* reported that someone travelling by car from Ash-

ford to Dover saw people in villages standing at their doors openly weeping for Grace Archer, and quoted a Londoner as saying: 'I thought I was in for a lively party when I was invited next door for the first night of ITV. Instead, it was like a house of mourning ...' A family in Romney were said to be collecting flowers to make into wreaths and crosses, and the BBC desperately appealed that 'no more flowers should be sent'. Letters of sympathy poured in for poor Phil: 'May I on behalf of my husband and my two neighbours say how sorry we are to hear of the death of your dear wife and with such tragic suddenness too' and one listener was moved to verse:

'A cruel death, it would not be denied,
That cut the bonds of love so lately tied.
I did not think the call would come so soon,
I found it night ere I thought it noon.'

The *Manchester Guardian*, too, was moved to verse – and in a parody of Wordsworth exposed what it thought was the real reason Grace had died:

A production meeting in the early 1950s. Producer Tony Shryane consults with programme assistant Valerie Hodgetts, secretary Hilary Evans, writer Edward J. Mason, and editor Godfrey Baseley.

Grace Archer
(*Dulce et decorum est pro BBC mori*)

She dwelt unseen, amid the Light,
Among the Archer clan,
And breathed her last the very night
The ITV began.

A maiden in a fantasy
All hidden from the eye –
A spoken word: the BBC
Decided she must die.

She was well-loved, and millions know
That Grace has ceased to be.
Now she is in her grave, but oh,
She's scooped the ITV.

M.C.

Others were less amused. The *News Chronicle* said: 'This was a silly, cheap, unworthy way of getting BBC publicity on the night ITV opened' and the *Daily Mail* demanded to know, as the listeners' fury mounted, 'Who are the guilty men?'

It soon provided the answer. 'These are the men who planned the death,' it said, and listed Denis Morris, Head of Midland Region Programmes; Rooney Pelletier, Controller Light Programmes; Tony Shyrane, the scriptwriters, and Godfrey Baseley.

The 'guilty men' were alarmed by the ferocity of the attacks, and the BBC called a hasty press conference in Birmingham and denied everything. The decision to kill Grace has been taken, it was explained, in order to reduce the number of characters ... to exploit the new situation created by the death of a major character ... because Ysanne Churchman was 'an accomplished artist' and the BBC wanted her to come back into the mainstream of broadcasting ....

Sadly, those were not the reasons at all. The written archives have since come to light, and the shocking truth can be told. At the June script meeting it was decided to kill a major character – precisely on the night ITV opened. Secretary Valerie Hodgetts was told not to duplicate and distribute minutes as usual, and a shortlist of victims was drawn up. On it were Christine Archer, Carol Grey, and newly-wed Grace. Grace was chosen. Somebody commented that Grace was not terribly popular with listeners because she was too independent and dis-

liked the idea of starting a family. The meeting agreed that Grace should endear herself to the nation again by changing her mind and rapidly becoming pregnant. The writers further agreed to twist the emotional knife still further by having her die trying to rescue a horse from a stables fire.

The secret was kept. To stop the cast from knowing anything they were spun a cunning yarn about scripts being written and recorded on the day as 'an exercise in topicality', and the first actress Ysanne Churchman knew about being written-out was when she arrived at Broadcasting House. The Press were invited to a special preview at 5 p.m., and there was, we are told, a stunned silence after Phil's final words: 'She's dead.' Then a quick-thinking newshound grabbed the nearest phone, dialled his paper, and demanded the newsdesk – only to find he was speaking into an unconnected studio prop.

So the Ambridge saga went on ... Blossom and Boxer had already made way for a smelly, nasty tractor; Ned Larkin took over from Simon, and Phil took up cine photography and became a boy scout leader. In 1957 he married cookery demonstrator Jill Patterson, and a year later they had twins, Shula

Drama in the studio for Bob Arnold and Norman Painting: in the script Tom Forrest had just killed Bob Larkin after a struggle in the dark in February 1957.

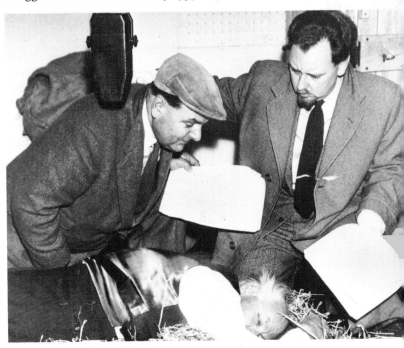

The famous 'Archers' continuity cards were started in 1951 and are maintained up to the present day.

and Kenton. In the 1960s new people came on the Ambridge scene, Jack Woolley and young Sidney Perks, and by the end of the decade John Tregorran had finally married Carol ... Jack eventually died in a Scottish sanatorium, and Doris quietly at home at Glebe Cottage.

More recently, there were complaints about sex when Nigel Pargetter tried to jump into Shula's bed, and profoundly shocked letters about declining standards when Brian was revealed having an affair with Caroline. But sensitive listeners are still soothed to hear about the life cycle of the warble fly, and comforted when Jill says 'One egg or two, Phil?' at breakfast time, and Peggy offers cups of tea at Blossom Hill Cottage. Walter doesn't say 'Me old pals me old beauties' as often as he used to, but Jethro has taken over from Ned, and he says 'My Eye!' very often indeed, and frequently demands to be allowed to lay a hedge 'in the old-fashioned way.'

We haven't changed all that much, and in one respect at least neither have our listeners. They like to believe Ambridge is *real* – just as they did when Godfrey Baseley invited them down the Worcestershire lanes in his 'mobile recording vehicle' back in December 1950. In the 1950s they wept for poor Grace, and in the 1960s sent baby clothes for Jennifer's illegitimate baby, Adam. In the 1970s, when Polly died, money was sent for a wreath, and one man phoned in tears after the funeral episode was broadcast. 'Did you send my wreath?' he asked, and when given an affirmative response: 'What sort of flowers were in it?' – a question that temporarily shook the person taking the call. When Doris died a woman wrote applying for the job of Dan's housekeeper, and when the children of Ambridge entered a national sunflower-growing contest a keen charity collector phoned asking if she could visit Ambridge to give the children a 'talk' about the project.

In more bizarre vein, Clarrie Grundy is firmly believed in by the computer of a national book club – it keeps writing to her at Grange Farm, Ambridge, demanding £44, and threatening to call in a debt collector. Records have arrived in the past, ordered, so the computerized print-out says, by Tony Archer of Bridge Farm. In shocking taste, a sex-magazine arrived for Phil Archer, Brookfield Farm, Ambridge, a couple of years ago.

Most people like to pretend – but some people just *know* that Ambridge is out there, just off the B3980, on the far side of Borsetshire's beautiful Hassett hills, an average English village going about its business just as it was on 1 January 1951.

The cast celebrate the twenty-first anniversary of the programme in December 1971.

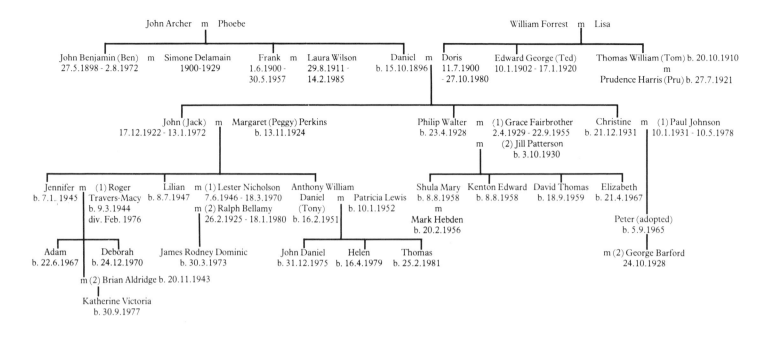

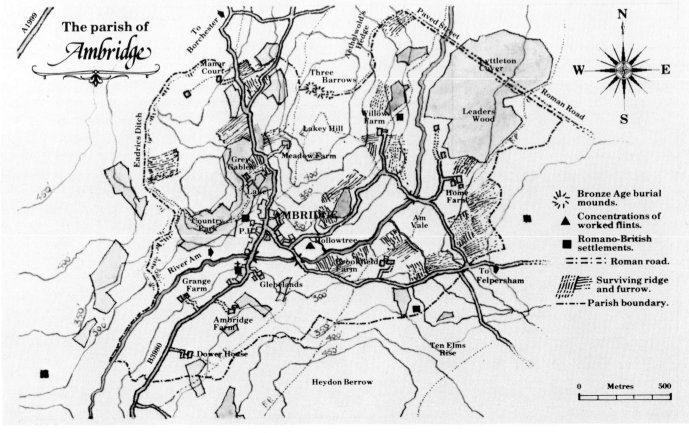

Above: Map of Ambridge.

The Listener's Guide to
AMBRIDGE

Ambridge is a village of about 360 inhabitants, six miles south of Borchester on the B3980. Its buildings are a mixture of thatched black-and-white timbered cottages, and houses in mellow brick and stone. Few buildings date from later than Victorian times. Exceptions are the police house (1931), twelve council houses (1955), six old people's bungalows at Manorfield Close (1961), the vicarage (1975), and a small development of high-quality private houses called 'Glebelands' built in the later 1970s.

The River Am runs through the village, and behind it the ground rises gently to Lakey Hill and beyond that to the Hassett Hills. From the summit of Lakey Hill you can see across the Vale of Am to the Malverns and, on a clear day, to the distant mountains of Wales. Other villages close by include Penny Hassett, Edgeley, Little Croxley, Loxley Barratt, Waterley Cross, and Netherbourne. Villages further away include Heybury, Perivale, Westbury, and Darrington.

The closest large town is Felpersham, which is seventeen miles away and has large department stores, some fine shops (including Laura Ashley, Austin Reed, and Habitat), a repertory theatre, and a crown court.

The nearest railway station is Hollerton Junction, which is just over two miles south of the village and is on the Inter-city Hereford-Paddington line. Trains usually take around two hours ten minutes to reach London, although the introduction of faster 125 trains in 1984 has helped speed up the service. There used to be a restaurant car on the 8.06 a.m. and 9.06 a.m. trains to London, but this was withdrawn some years ago.

There is a splendid wooden bus shelter in the village, but there are no bus services except for the school bus, which takes primary and secondary pupils to Borchester. The only way to get to Borchester by public transport is to walk one and a half miles to the A1999 Borchester-Hollerton road (the old Borchester Turnpike) and get a bus from Wharton's Garage. In the late 1970s, Ambridge and Penny Hassett took part in the GPO's 'postbus' experiment, but in this area at least it was deemed unsuccessful and a normal van was restored in 1980.

Opposite above: A tranquil tea-time at Brookfield Farm, 1951. But life for most of the Archer family was far from peaceful. Jack, looking wistfully at the jam tarts, was doing badly with his smallholding. Christine was having trouble with Dick Raymond, reporter on the *Borchester Echo*, and Phil had been turned down by Grace Fairbrother. Dan, however, had every reason to look smug. He was about to be made vice-president of the Ambridge tennis club. June Spencer (Peggy), Denis Folwell (Jack), Gwen Berryman (Doris), Pamela Mant (Christine), Norman Painting (Philip). *Opposite below*: At twenty-two Phil was already a farm manager, and proud to be earning one pound a week more than the national average. He got on better, however, with his employer Mr Fairbrother than he did with Grace. Monica Grey (Grace), Leslie Bowmar (Mr Fairbrother).

Above: While Dan reads his paper and Doris darns socks, Christine studies the National Milk Records. Her thoughts, though, were with the mineralogist Keith Latimer, who had replaced Dick Raymond in her affections, and taken her to see *Tilly of Bloomsbury* in Borchester.

Peggy's mother, Mrs Perkins, moved to Ambridge in 1951. Doris introduced her to country life, and showed her where eggs came from. Pauline Seville (Mrs Perkins).

In the Village

Facing the village green is **The Bull,** which is a free house owned by Peggy Archer. The licensee is Sid Perks, whose wife Polly died in a road accident in 1982. Their daughter Lucy is now fourteen.

The Bull is a black-and-white timbered hostelry dating for the most part from the late-seventeenth century, although the back of the building is said to be even older. (A ghost who 'taps' on a back bedroom window is reputed to be that of a drummer boy from the Civil War.) The pub has two bars, the Public and the Ploughman's and there is also a small room, the Snug, next to the public bar. The Bull sells the highly-acclaimed Shire's best bitter, a traditional ale from the Borchester Brewery. Food is served both at lunchtime and in the evening, but it is less ambitious than it was when Polly was alive, or when Caroline Bone (who now works at Grey Gables) was serving *cordon bleu* meals in the Plough-

Walter Gabriel gives Dan his opinion on a cow which was entered for the Borchester Show. Robert Mawdesley (Walter).

man's some five years ago. Nowadays it is mainly bar snacks: bread and cheese, hot pies and pizzas, chicken or scampi and chips. . . .

The Bull has five guest bedrooms, but the bed-and-breakfast trade has also fallen away considerably since Polly died. There is a decent-sized upstairs function room with an old piano in it. (The piano was donated to The Bull by the Grundys in 1984, after Eddie had ruined the existing piano by being sick in it.)

Part-time barmaids are Susan Carter and Clarrie Grundy, and the part-time barman is Fred Lamb from Penny Hassett.

The Bull has had a darts team (Winter League) for many years, and there is keen rivalry every December when the local derby is played against the team from the Cat and Fiddle at Edgeley. A trophy was presented several years ago by Mrs Lilian Bellamy, and is currently in the possession of the Cat and Fiddle.

Sid Perks owns a cottage at Penny Hassett, **Rose Cottage**, which he and Polly bought as a permanent home but never lived in. At the moment it is let to Kathy Holland.

At the top end of the Green, on the same side of the road as The Bull, is the **Village Hall**, which was built in 1920 and has a main room and also a small kitchen used for preparing tea and biscuits and sandwiches. The kitchen was modernized after a fire in 1977, and has a gleaming electric tea urn and a plentiful supply of willow-pattern plates and teacups and saucers.

At one end of the hall is a stage, and at the other is an old billiards table that was once the pride and joy of the (now defunct) Ambridge Men's Club. There is a carved-oak war memorial board set into one wall. It lists twenty-four names under 1914-18: Archers, Blowers, Forrests, and Gabriels feature strongly, most of them privates or NCOs in the 5th Battalion, The Borsetshire Regiment.

The hall also has chairs and trestle tables, and a notice board which has on it flyblown certificates telling how Ambridge WI came second, third, or 'commended' in county drama competitions in the 1950s.

The hall is principally used by the Playgroup (run every morning, Monday to Friday, by Dorothy Adamson and helpers), and by the Over Sixties, who

Dan takes a drop of 'something special' to the calves.

meet here once a week. Laura Archer was the organizer of the Over Sixties (who have an 'outing', usually to Weston-super-Mare, every September, and a party every Christmas), but this job has now been taken over by Peggy Archer.

The Parish Council meets in the hall once a month, and it is also used for jumble sales, whist drives, wedding receptions, and birthday parties. It is the venue for the Flower and Produce Show, the Harvest Supper, Conservative Association whist drives, and the Christmas Concert.

The hall is run by a sub-committee of the Parish Council, who are anxious to encourage more people to use the facilities available.

South of the main village, on a slight rise of land just over the River Am, is **the parish church of St Stephen's**. It was consecrated in 1281 and dedicated ten years later. Architecturally, it is a combination of Saxon, late Norman, and Early English and Perpendicular styles.

The font is very interesting, being octagonal, very ornate, and enriched with carved human heads and flowers. It is believed to have been a gift to the church by Edward I, and the heads are thought to be those of the King and Queen Eleanor of Castille.

The Lawson Chapel, or South Transept, was added in the early sixteenth century. It contains the alabaster tomb of Richard Lawson (who bought the manors of Ambridge and Lyttleton in 1472) and his wife Ann. It also contains a tablet in memory of 'Black Lawson', the squire of Ambridge who fell from his horse and broke his neck on Lady Day 1697, and whose ghost is said to ride still across Heydon Berrow, accompanied by two hell hounds who follow him till dawn.

In the chancel there is the Woolhay Memorial, a tablet uncovered some years ago and relating to the ancient Woolhay family of Lyttleton. Jack Woolley believes that his own family (although long established in Stirchley, Birmingham) is a junior branch of the Woolhay line.

The church tower is fifty-six feet high, and leans over six inches to the west. The six bells were re-hung in 1975.

The church guttering was replaced in the early 1980s, and the organ massively restored after having been largely eaten by church mice during the winter months. The churchyard was levelled in 1984, and many of the old gravestones placed round the edges of the yard and the paths. Inscriptions of interest include:

All you that do this way pafs by,
As you are now, fo once was I.
As I am now fo fhalt you be,
Therefore prepare to follow me.

E. Blower, 1710

My anvil and hammer lies declined,
My bellows have quite lost their wind,
My fire's extinct, my forge decay'd,
My vice is in the dust all laid.
My coals is spent, my iron is gone,

Life was hard for Jack and Peggy. She was in hospital for several weeks with diptheria, and when she came out was distressed to hear rumours about Jack and village schoolmistress Elsie Catcher. Then Jack went into the county hospital for nervous and mental disorders for four months. Thelma Rogers (Peggy).

My mortal parts rest nigh this stone,
My soul to heaven, I hope is gone.

Thomas Salter, Blacksmith of
Ambridge, d. 12 June 1784

The vicar of Ambridge (who is also rector of Penny Hassett and vicar of Edgeley) is Richard Adamson.

The churchwardens at St Stephen's are Tom Forrest and Jill Archer. The monthly parish magazine (called *The Link*) is edited by Mrs Antrobus.

Right: Tom Forrest admires Phil's labrador dog Topsy. Tom was having a bad time in 1953 – after being hurt in a fight with a poacher, a fire broke out in the Squire's wood and Tom had to evacuate his cottage and move his dogs to Brookfield. Phil was also having a difficult time. At the Coronation bonfire on Lakey Hill, Grace told him she was going to Ireland for a year to train in horse management, and they quarrelled bitterly at her farewell party at the Country Club. Bob Arnold (Tom Forrest).

Below: teatime at Brookfield, 1954, and while Phil ponders over his *Pig-breeder's Weekly*, Christine studies her future in the tea-leaves. In the spring she was romantically involved with the Squire's nephew, Clive Lawson-Hope, and in March he proposed to her. Christine turned him down, and he went off to Africa.

Above: milking time at Brookfield, March 1954.

Above: Life was one long struggle for Ambridge's inefficient, down-at-heel smallholder Walter Gabriel. He dug his midden and toiled with his calves, but the Squire's nephew Clive Lawson-Hope was determined to drive him out of his 40-acre farm. Walter fared little better in his affection for Mrs. P. He showed her his rusting implements (*right*), but she remained suspicious about his motives.

Turning back towards the village, past the old chestnut trees in the vicarage garden, is a small house of mellow bricks called **Glebe Cottage**. It was built around 1840 and is now the home of Dan Archer. It has three downstairs rooms, a sitting-room (containing a grandfather clock), a kitchen, and a large hall which was also used as a dining-room when Doris was alive; and two bedrooms and a bathroom upstairs. It has a fine glass conservatory built when Dan and Doris retired from Brookfield in 1970, and a garden with a vegetable plot.

Opposite Glebe Cottage is a development of eight modern houses, each with four bedrooms, two bathrooms and a patio, called **Glebelands**. The nearest house to the road is occupied by the Fletcher family.

Back over the bridge and into the village proper is **the village shop**. This is owned by Jack Woolley

and run by Martha Woodford, a widow whose husband Joby was a woodman on the Ambridge Estate. Dorothy Adamson also works part time in the shop, which sells mainly foodstuffs, tobacco, sweets, newspapers and magazines, polish, detergents, etc. This is also a post office counter. The shop closes for lunch between 1 p.m. and 2 p.m. Half-day closing is on a Thursday.

On the far side of the village green, beyond the duck pond and shielded behind an evergreen hedge, are the **Manorfield Close** old folks' bungalows. No. 2 is occupied by Mrs Perkins, and No. 3 by Mrs Bagshawe. **The council houses** are also on the far

side of the green. They are semi-detached and each has a good vegetable plot at the back and a flower garden at the front. The Horobins live at No. 1 (where the flower garden is used to park ageing and expired Morris Marinas, rusty old Vauxhalls, and oil-leaking Renaults). At number six ('Dunroamin') live Neil and Susan Carter with their daughter Emma.

To the north of the green, on the opposite side of the B3980 to the Village Hall, is *Honeysuckle Cottage*. This is a black-and-white thatched building with an old English garden. It has a living-room and kitchen downstairs, and a bedroom and bathroom upstairs. It is the home of Walter Gabriel and, occasionally, of his son Nelson. In the mid-1970s Nelson (then an entrepreneur in London) had the loft boarded so that he could store packages and crates in it.

Woodbine Cottage, the home of Jethro Larkin,

also overlooks the green, and the *Police House* (now owned by Detective Sergeant Dave Barry) is close by. The police house has recently had pine-cladding fitted to one wall of the kitchen, which is painted bright yellow.

The Stables, away from the centre of the village, is a house with riding stables and an indoor riding school next to it. The house, and business, was bought by Ambridge Farmers as a home for Christine Johnson when her husband Paul died in 1977. Christine married gamekeeper George Barford the following year, and they now live in the house together. *Manor Court* is the home of John and Carol Tregorran, and is a fine eighteenth-century gentleman's house on three acres. Carol also runs a market garden with two large glasshouses, and a two-acre vineyard.

The small village garage, which used to be owned by Haydn Evans, closed down in 1985.

Around the Village

At the end of a farm track leading from the Netherbourne and Little Croxley road is **Brookfield Farm**, the home of Phil and Jill Archer, their son David, and their daughter Elizabeth.

Brookfield is in the centre of one of Ambridge's four medieval fields, but the farm itself is a late seventeenth-century building, part stone and part black-and-white. It has five bedrooms and two bathrooms (the second was added in 1985 and is *en suite* with one of the bedrooms). There is also a downstairs WC and washroom. The kitchen was newly fitted in 1982 with a blue Aga, a wall-phone, pine units, a built-in oven and grill, and a dishwasher. Visitors can come straight into the kitchen, via a porch, from the farmyard. The sitting-room has a stereo system and a piano (which Phil plays well and Elizabeth not very well) and there is a fireplace which burns logs throughout the winter. The farm office is small, looks out on the farmyard, and has

Life cheered up for Jack and Peggy when they were given the tenancy of The Bull by Stourhampton Brewery. Jack told his wife about pouring bottled beer (*below*), and (*opposite*) about pruning the roses in The Bull's beer garden.

doors both straight to the yard and into the house.

Brookfield has been the home of the Archer family for many generations. In late-Victorian times it was owned by the Lawson-Hope estate and the tenant was John Archer, who married a farmer's daughter called Phoebe from Edgeley. They had three sons, Ben, Daniel, and Frank. In the course of time, Ben emigrated to Canada and Frank to New Zealand, and it was Dan Archer who took over the tenancy of Brookfield and married Doris Forrest, the daughter of a gamekeeper on the Squire's estate.

Doris gave birth to two sons, Jack and Philip, and a daughter, Christine. Jack is now dead, Christine is married to gamekeeper George Barford, and Phil Archer is running Brookfield.

Across the River Am the ground rises up to Lakey Hill and Brookfield land gives way to Home Farm pasture, and to the few acres of land that still surround the old farmhouse of **Willow Farm**. Bill Insley bought the farmhouse when the farm was sold by Haydn Evans, and he lets Neil Carter use a couple of the old farm buildings for his battery hens and deep-litter birds. Willow farmhouse itself is an unattractive red-brick building with ivy covering the front wall.

The view from Willow Farm is delightful, looking south east to Leader's Wood and the rolling acres of **Home Farm,** with the River Am winding its way down the valley and the dense woodland of Long Wood and Lyttleton Cover rising beyond. Home Farm is built on the foundations of the ancient Lyttleton Manor, which was destroyed by fire in 1701. It is therefore principally early eighteenth century in origin. After the Second World War it was converted to superior luxury flats and the land round it was farmed as part of the Bellamy Estate. It was converted back again into a house by Brian Aldridge, a rich thirty-two-year-old bachelor, who bought the buildings and 1,500 acres in 1975. Brian married Jennifer Travers-Macy in 1976.

Dan's shepherd, Len Thomas, takes a hand at tractor driving. Arnold Peters (Len Thomas).

The kitchen at Home Farm is superbly equipped with English Rose oak units, and there is an Aga. There is a children's playroom with a blackboard built into the wall. The sitting-room has a splendid inglenook fireplace. The dining-room looks out on to the lawns and rose garden. Outside there is a modern swimming pool and a barbecue. There is a small paddock by the house where Jennifer keeps her small flock of Jacob sheep.

Away from the house, in what used to be an old barn, is Jennifer's 'studio'. Here the stonework has been painted white and has upon it spotlights and colourful ethnic rugs. There are electric storage heaters and a spinning wheel stands in one corner.

Jennifer's son Adam has just left Sherborne School, but is not yet living at home; her daughter Debbie is at Cheltenham Ladies' College; Kate goes to a private preparatory school some eight miles away and Jennifer is involved every day with the 'school run' – sharing transport with the parents of other children at the school.

Bridge Farm is late-nineteenth century with the farm buildings built on to the side of the farmhouse. The high ceilings and old sash windows make for many cold draughts in winter. The kitchen has plastic-topped units and a rather elderly Rayburn stove. The farm is 140 acres, on one side adjoining Home Farm and on the other Heydon Berrow and Ten Elms Rise. The 'bridge' in the farm's name no longer exists – it used to carry the Little Croxley road over Heydon Brook, but the brook now runs through a culvert under the metalled road.

Bridge Farm is part of the Bellamy Estate and is rented by Lilian Bellamy's brother, Tony Archer, and his wife Pat. They have been there now for seven years and are in the process of 'going organic' by stopping using artificial fertilizers and pesticides on their land. In 1985 they harvested their first organic crops – ten acres devoted to wheat, potatoes, and carrots – and had mixed success.

The farm has a good herringbone milking parlour, and an excellent covered silage clamp.

Pat and Tony have three children, John, Helen, and Thomas. Each morning Pat has to take John and Helen to catch the school bus, and Thomas to the playgroup. Later in the day she has to collect them. The family has a pet dog, a cross between a golden retriever and a labrador, called Bessie.

South of Ambridge, beyond Glebelands and the parish church, is **Ambridge Farm**. This is rented from the Bellamy Estate by Mike Tucker and his wife Betty. They are unusual for the Ambridge area in having a herd of Ayrshire cows rather than Friesians. Mike also has a milk round (although he no longer bottles his own milk) and Betty has tried to run a farm shop but found it too much for her. The Tuckers have two children, Roy and Brenda.

Adjoining Ambridge Farm, between the Hollerton road and the River Am, is **Grange Farm**, also rented from the Bellamy Estate. Grange Farm is

Inspecting the stock at Brookfield in 1954 – Phil, Simon, Mr Fairbrother, and Dan. Leslie Bowmar (Mr Fairbrother), Harry Oakes (Dan).

built on eighteenth-century foundations and is a mixture of stone, crumbling brick and cement rendering which is cracked, stained, and falling away from the front wall of the house in chunks. There is an old solid-fuel stove in the kitchen, which also has an orange plastic-tiled floor, an old-fashioned enamelled kitchen sink, brown-painted cupboards on the walls, and a glass-fronted 'kitchenette' unit bought in 1958. Cooking is done either on the stove or on an old electric cooker. During the evenings the tenant, Joe Grundy, sits in his father's old wooden chair by the stove (if it is lit) or goes into the parlour. Here there is a fireplace, with 1937-design tiles round it, but the chimney smokes badly and he uses a one-bar electric fire.

Joe works Grange Farm with his younger son, Eddie, and his daughter-in-law Clarrie. Eddie has converted the cellar into a 'Country and Western' shrine, and has painted herds of bison (crossing the plains of Wyoming) on the walls. He likes to sit in the cellar drinking home-made cider and listening to Dolly Parton on his stereo.

Outside the house there is an area of ground that Clarrie has been struggling, for two or three years now, to turn into a garden. There is also the turkey shed, where Joe raises around fifty turkeys every autumn, and where Grange Farm celebrations used

Walter and Simon having a pint and a game of dominoes.

to be held in days gone by. It was last decked out with bunting in 1979 when Eddie was getting married to Dolly Treadgold. The wedding, however, was called off and the party cancelled.

Across the River Am from Grange Farm is the Ambridge Country Park with its nature trails, information centre, and herd of fallow deer; and in the centre of the park is Arkwright Lake. The park (which attracts many visitors and school parties in the summer) is next to **Grey Gables Country House Hotel**, and both are owned by former Birmingham businessman Jack Woolley. Grey Gables also owns a large part of Lyttleton Cover, and offers syndicate shooting by the day in winter and riding holidays in the summer. There is also a garden centre managed by Jim Bolton and a small golf course with its own club house and bar.

Grey Gables itself is a late-Victorian Gothic mansion set in fifteen acres of lawns and gardens and noted for its fine chestnut trees. There are twenty-four bedrooms (each with private bathroom), a restaurant, cocktail bar, lounge bar, and banqueting hall. There is a ground floor 'garden suite', which is occupied by Jack Woolley's assistant Caroline Bone.

Staff at Grey Gables include a hotel manager called Hartshorne, a chef called Jean-Paul (famous for his French tartlets), an assistant restaurant manageress called Trudy Porter, a secretary/receptionist called Fiona, and Higgs the handiman. Higgs also doubles as Jack Woolley's chauffeur when Jack uses his Bentley, and he grows famous prize chrysanthemums in the hothouse.

The Ambridge cricket pitch, with clubhouse, is on Grey Gables land donated by Jack Woolley, and there is a new outdoor swimming pool at the hotel.

Behind the Country Park and golf course is Blossom Hill, and **Blossom Hill Cottage** is the home of Peggy Archer and her cat Sammy. The cottage was severely damaged by fire two years ago, and rebuilding work took several months. The cottage

Everything was going nicely for Phil. His pig-breeding scheme was prospering (as he explained to his father *below*) and Grace had come home from Ireland and agreed to marry him.

has two bedrooms, and a pleasant sitting-room with french windows leading out to the garden.

Ambridge Hall is a Victorian edifice, built by an enlightened squire, John Lawson-Hope, for the use of a resident village doctor. It must have been an eyesore in 1860, but now the yellow bricks and green tiles have mellowed, there are attractive wooden shutters on the windows, and mature beech and willow trees in the two acres of garden. It is a big house, with six bedrooms, and it is very hard to heat properly in the winter. There is a rather good glass sunhouse, now disused, and outhouses used for keeping goats, ducks, hens, and pet lambs from time to time. There is a splendid fruit garden, and the lawns run down to the River Am. In the summer, croquet is played on the front lawn.

In her famous black-feathered hat, Mrs Perkins discusses Jennifer's school report with Peggy and Jack.

Ambridge Hall was the home of Laura Archer, the widow of Frank Archer of Brookfield Farm, and for many years she lived with Colonel Freddie Danby as her paying guest. In the spring of 1985 she died, without having signed her will (which left the property to Freddie), and after several months Ambridge Hall was inherited by a twenty-two-year-old great niece from South Otago, New Zealand, called Judy Cameron.

Set back from the Netherbourne and Little Croxley road is **Nightingale Farm** which was used as a rural Arts and Crafts Centre until 1975, and then as a village youth club for two or three years. The farmland was sold long ago, but the house still has a useful range of outbuildings and four acres of garden and paddock. The owner was Hugo Barnaby and until Christmas 1984 Neil Carter and his wife Susan lived in the two-bedroom upstairs flat. When they left, the house was put on the market and sold to Mrs Marjorie Antrobus, a breeder and shower of Afghan hounds. Soon after, she moved in (having restored the downstairs rooms to their original state) and let the upstairs flat to Nigel Pargetter.

Phil's first love, the beautiful Grace Fairbrother, who married him in 1955 after a tempestuous courtship. Only a few months later Phil was offered a directorship by Grace's father, and gave a dinner at Grey Gables to celebrate. During the evening the stables caught fire, and in trying to rescue *Midnight* Grace was injured by a falling beam. She died in Phil's arms on the way to hospital. Ysanne Churchman (Grace Fairbrother).

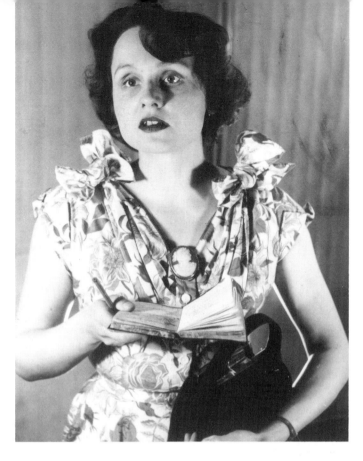

Who is Doing What

Parish Council (Elected 1983, due for re-election in 1987). CHAIRMAN: Colonel Danby. MEMBERS: Peggy Archer, Jack Woolley, Jean Harvey, Dorothy Adamson, Christine Barford, Tony Archer. The post of clerk has been left unfilled since Haydn Evans left the parish.
Parochial Church Council (Elected yearly, between Easter and 30 April). CHURCHWARDENS: Jill Archer, Tom Forrest. MEMBERS: Jean Harvey, Carol Tregorran, Brian Aldridge, Derek Fletcher. The vacancy caused by the death of Laura Archer has been filled by Phil Archer.
Village Hall Committee (A sub-committee of the Parish Council): Dorothy Adamson, Jean Harvey, Colonel Danby. Bookings for the Hall are done through Jean Harvey at Bull Farm.
Bellringing team: Shula Archer, George Barford, Christine Barford, Tom Forrest, Neil Carter.
CHURCH ORGANIST: Phil Archer

The Bull darts team (This varies, but the team is chosen from the following): Neil Carter (Captain), David Archer, Mike Tucker, Sid Perks, Eddie Grundy (when not playing for the Cat and Fiddle), Stuart Horobin, Tom Forrest.
Cricket team: In 1984 and 1985 David Archer was captain. Other players included: Sid Perks, Brian Aldridge, Nelson Gabriel, Neil Carter, Stuart Horobin, Richard Adamson, and Nigel Pargetter.
WRVS organizer locally is Jill Archer, and Jennifer Aldridge also helps her with meals-on-wheels. Peggy Archer is an organizer for the Church of England *Children's Society*. Shula Archer is on the committee of Borchester *Young Conservatives*, and Pat Archer is an active member of *Borchester CND* and several 'Women's Groups' in the area.

For a time in 1985 Eddie Grundy was treasurer of Borchester *Country and Western Club*, but he was asked to resign in September.

Ambridge in History

On Lakey Hill a group of three barrows or burial mounds of **Bronze Age** date can still be seen, although these have been much reduced by ploughing since the Second World War and are now about a metre high. In 1981 a large number of flint fragments were found in 'Long Ground', a field next to the Hollowtree Pig Unit. They included some half-dozen microliths (tiny flint blades used by Mesolithic peoples around 7000–5000 BC), two leaf-shaped arrowheads of Neolithic date (*c.* 3000–2000 BC) and several Bronze Age barbed and tanged arrowheads.

It is known that in AD 46, three years after the **Roman invasion** of Britain under Emperor Claudius, the XIVth Legion crossed the line of what was to become the Fosse Way, and overran the native tribes of Borsetshire. From then until the early fifth century the county was a settled and prosperous part of the Roman Empire. In Ambridge one Romano-British site at Jiggin's Field has been known about since the accidental discovery of quantities of pottery there during the cutting of a new drainage ditch in the 1880s. The site was partly excavated in 1975–6 due to the threat of deep ploughing, and evidence of a Roman farmstead was revealed.

The administration of the Borchester area was based in the tribal capital of the Dubunni at Cirencester (Corinium), but Borchester was an important trading post and a major Roman road (now the A1999) ran north through the town from Akeman Street to Droitwich, passing within a mile and a half of the Ambridge settlement.

Reasonable information about **Saxon Ambridge** is contained in a charter covering the grant of an estate of six hides of land in Ambridge to the wealthy monastery of St Mary in Worcester. The land was granted in 936 by Athelstan, third of the great West Saxon kings, and in return the monks were asked to pray for an English victory over the Celtic, Danish, and Norwegian forces massing in northern Britain. Athelstan's charter covers only

land north of the river: there was a further estate of four hides around what is now Grange Farm. This was also in the hands of the monks of St Mary's, Worcester, at the time of the **Domesday Survey** – as the entry of Ambridge shows:

> The Prior of St Mary's, Worcester, holds Ambridge with one berewick. Eadred holds it of him. There are ten hides. There are four ploughlands in demesne with 8 serfs. Eight villeins, 12 bordars, and 2 cottars have 12 ploughs. There is woodland 3 leagues by half a league and five acres of meadow. There is a mill rendering 200 eels annually. In the time of King Edward it was worth 80 shillings, and now 100 shillings.

Later documentary evidence shows that by the later Middle Ages Ambridge had four open fields: West Field, Lakey Hill Field, East Field, and Brook Field (the name of the last survives in the name Brookfield Farm). It was not, however, until a parish survey was undertaken in 1980 that evidence of a deserted medieval village of Ambridge (the berewick of the Domesday Survey, presumably) was discovered. Aerial photographs showed a medieval village site at Grange Farm, and a blocked stone tracery window of Norman origin was found in the wall of a Grange Farm barn. Further research at the Public Record Office by Jennifer Aldridge and John Tregorran showed that the Grange Farm settlement had passed to the Cistercian Abbey of Darrington during the thirteenth century, and that the inhabitants had been dispossessed to make way for a vast flock of sheep.

There are several houses in the parish that go back to **Tudor times**, the most notable being Manor Court with its small minstrels' gallery and Wynfords with its paved Elizabethan courtyard. There are no famous Tudor figures connected with the village, although Penny Hassett is proud to have been the home of the poet and adventurer Sir Sidney Cook, the man who devised the little-known 'Borsetshire Sonnet'. It is fondly (and very firmly) believed that Shakespeare visited Ambridge and stayed at The Bull, but the only evidence for this is that an old Ambridge word 'biggen', meaning a child's cap, is found in Henry IV part 2 (Act IV Scene iv): 'Whose brow with homely biggen bound'.

At the time of The **Civil War** the squire of Ambridge was Thomas Lawson, Esq, and on 3 September 1642, he marched to Nottingham, where the King had raised the Royal Standard, and took with him two of his tenants, a Blower and a Gabriel. Three weeks after he had gone, Ambridge saw the only hostilities that were to take place in the area during the war. On 27 September an army under the Earl of Essex billeted itself on Churcham, and the next day passed through Leyton Cross and reached Borchester in the evening. In his 'Letters from a Subaltern Officer of the Earl of Essex's Army' Nehemiah Cook described Borchester as 'a very malignant towne', and he also described a brief engagement which took place the following day at Hassett Bridge, north of Lakey Hill, when Essex's

troops encountered a detachment of Royalists under the Earl of Northampton:

> Our gunner tooke their owne bullet, sent it to them againe, and killed a horse and a man, wherupon all their foote companies fled and offered ther armes in Hollerton and Hassett for twelve pence a peece. Ther troopes whelinge about toke up ther dead bodies, but the horse they left behind, some of them having their guts beaten out on both sides. One drumner beinge dead at the bottome of the hill our knap sack boyes rifled to the shirt, which was very lowzy. Another drumner wee found in the inn at Ambrige, with his arme shot off, and lay a dieinge.

There is a persistent belief in a ghost at The Bull, said to be that of a drummer boy tapping at an upstairs window and asking to be let in. Perhaps, though, the 'tapping' is really the beat of a ghostly drum.

Squire Lawson returned to Ambridge in 1644, when he was one of the tax commissioners who took the August tax-gathering for Borsetshire to the King in Oxford. In 1649, after the ending of the first Civil War, he 'compounded' with parliament and was

The first bus service to Ambridge started in 1904 and was run by the Borchester and District Motor Omnibus Company.

Morris dancers from Perivale outside The Bull in 1890.
Morris dancers still perform on Ambridge village green every
Spring Bank Holiday.

allowed to keep his estate on payment of a fine of
£4,000.

The only relic of the Civil War found in Ambridge is a stone cannonball, discovered many years
ago in the roots of a dead laurel bush by Walter
Gabriel.

By early Victorian times Ambridge was a re-
latively prosperous and very self-contained community which milled the corn grown in its own
fields, baked its own bread and brewed its own ale.
It made its own furniture and tools, its carts, field-
gates, coffins and cribs, its boots and smocks. Children were taught at the village school and the village
church. The village shop sold food the cottagers
could not make or grow themselves: salt, pepper,
and tea, and large quantities of cheese and treacle as
well as working clothes and patent medicines. In

1850 the History, Gazetteer and Directory of Borsetshire listed Ambridge as:

A parish and pleasant village five miles south of Borchester. It contains 2,210 acres of land. In 1841 the
parish rates were £441.11.2d. at 6s.6d. in the pound.
The abbot of St Mary's, Worcester, was an early pos-
sessor of the lordship, which now resides with the
Lawson-Hope family. A carrier calls on Thursday from
Hollerton to Borchester, and returns.

Directory
Blower T. Baker and miller
Box R. Shoemaker
Clarke T. Shopkeeper
Hands R. Hurdlemaker
Morris J. Schoolmaster
Mumford R. Carpenter
Perrin S. Publican and maltster
Rev Richard Leadbeater, Vicar
Slatter J. Carpenter
Gabriel J. Blacksmith
Waters C. Farrier
Rouse J. Wheelwright.

Who is Farming What

Brookfield extends to 508 acres and is very much a traditional 'mixed' farm, with cows, pigs, sheep, and corn. The dairy herd numbers around 100 friesians (it was bigger before quotas came in) and there are around 80 followers – heifers being raised to join the herd, and bull calves being raised for beef. The pig unit is based at Hollowtree, in the buildings of the old Victorian farm, and sixty sows produce offspring that are sold as baconers. There are four boars at the unit, and the senior one is always known as 'Playboy'. On Lakey Hill and the pasture round the old Marney's farm is the flock of 300 ewes (mainly a cross-breed known as 'mules'). Round the farmhouse at Brookfield there are usually a couple of dozen free-range hens producing eggs.

There are over 250 acres of grass (grazing, hay, and silage) and nearly 200 acres of cereals (mainly winter wheat and barley) and there are 50 acres of oilseed rape and 16 acres of potatoes.

Working the farm are Phil Archer (manager and relief worker); Graham Collard (cowman); Jethro Larkin (general); Neil Carter (mainly pigs); and David Archer (assistant manager and general).

Home Farm covers 1,500 acres and is mainly arable, although there is a flock of 600 ewes (200 lambing in January; 400 in March and April) and a beef unit which has 30 suckler cows that rear around 150 calves each year. There are generally around 120 beef cattle on the farm, together with a Limousin bull. Cereals, though, dominate the farm's economy – 900 acres of wheat and barley, together with 150 acres of oilseed rape, 100 acres of grassland, and 80 acres of woodland.

Working the farm are Brian Aldridge (manager and relief worker); Steve Manson (working foreman); Sammy Whipple (cattle and sheep); three tractor drivers; one boy.

Bridge Farm includes 140 acres rented from the Bellamy estate and ten acres of accommodation land near the village. It is mainly dairy – in 1984 there were 95 milkers (Friesians) and 55 followers, and apart from 25 acres of barley the farm was devoted entirely to grassland. In late 1984, however, Tony Archer and his wife Pat decided to 'go organic' by cutting out artificial fertilizers, herbicides, and pesticides on their land. As a first step (and because of quotas) they cut the dairy herd and dismissed their full-time worker Malcolm Lewis. In 1985 they grew 10 acres of organic wheat, carrots, and potatoes. The intention is to devote 20 per cent of the farm to 'organic production' each year until the land is entirely converted. Pat Archer still keeps around 100 hens on a free-range system.

Working the farm are Tony Archer, Pat (part-time) and contract labour for silage making and harvest. Retired farmer Percy Jordan was a regular helper until his death in August 1985.

Ambridge Farm extends to 150 acres rented from the Bellamy estate and 15 acres rented from Gavin Fry. There are 65 Ayrshires in the dairy herd, and 35 followers. Apart from grassland, there are around 60 acres of cereals. Mike and Betty Tucker also run a milk round – they used to bottle their own 'green top' milk, but their bottling plant became unreliable and milk is now supplied ready bottled by Borchester Dairies.

Working the farm are Mike Tucker, Betty (part-time), Stuart Horobin, and some contract labour.

Grange Farm covers 120 acres, entirely rented from the Bellamy Estate. There are around 35 Friesians in the dairy herd, and between 15 and 20 followers depending on the general financial state of the farm. Pigs and turkeys are reared on a small scale. Otherwise the farm is devoted to cereals – winter wheat on land that can be ploughed and drilled in time, and spring barley on the rest – and enough grassland to provide grazing, hay, and silage for the livestock.

Working the farm are Joe Grundy and Eddie Grundy (who also does contract labour on other farms and sells loads of logs, scrap metal, etc).

Dan offers a mouthful of hay to *Midnight*, the horse that was rescued from the stables fire. Christine was now married to the dashing horse-owner Paul Johnson.

Opposite above: Carol Grey spent most of the 1950s having a remarkable friendship with the wild and romantic John Tregorran, who appeared in Ambridge with a green caravan in 1953, and proposed to Carol a week or so later. But although she regarded John with fond affection, she eventually married suave, bearded businessman Charles Grenville, who had bought the Fairbrother Estate. Anne Cullen (Carol Grey), Michael Shaw (Charles Grenville).

Opposite below: Dan and Phil inspecting the Brookfield bullocks. 1958 was a hard year on the farm – Dan lost most of his oats when fire broke out in his dutch barn.

A year after marrying Phil quietly in Crudley Church, Jill gave birth to twins – and Dan was bewildered to find he had grandchildren called Kenton and Shula. Patricia Greene (Jill).

Opposite above: Sunday afternoon at Brookfield Farm, and Dan and Doris are at the gate to welcome Jack and Peggy, with their two daughters Jennifer and Lilian. Thelma Rogers (Peggy), Freda Hooper (Jennifer), Margaret Lane (Lilian).

Opposite below: the Ambridge Fête, 1959. Holding a candlestick from the white elephant stall is businessman Charles Grenville, in the deckchair is Mrs Turvey, and on the far left inspecting the bottom of a jug is Charles Grenville's mysterious housekeeper Madame Garonne, who turned out, in due course, to be an international drug smuggler. Irene Prador (Mme Garonne), Michael Shaw (Charles Grenville), Courtney Hope (Mrs Turvey).

Ned Larkin in rumbustious mood. Bill Payne (Ned Larkin).

Opposite above: Tom, Walter, and Dan at bellringing practice, 1959.

Opposite below: Dan got a new dairyman at Brookfield – the charming Irishman Paddy Redmond, seen here inspecting the herd. Paddy was later to take more interest in young Jennifer Archer from The Bull – and to get her pregnant before quarrelling with Phil over a milk bonus scheme and leaving Ambridge. John Bott (Paddy Redmond).

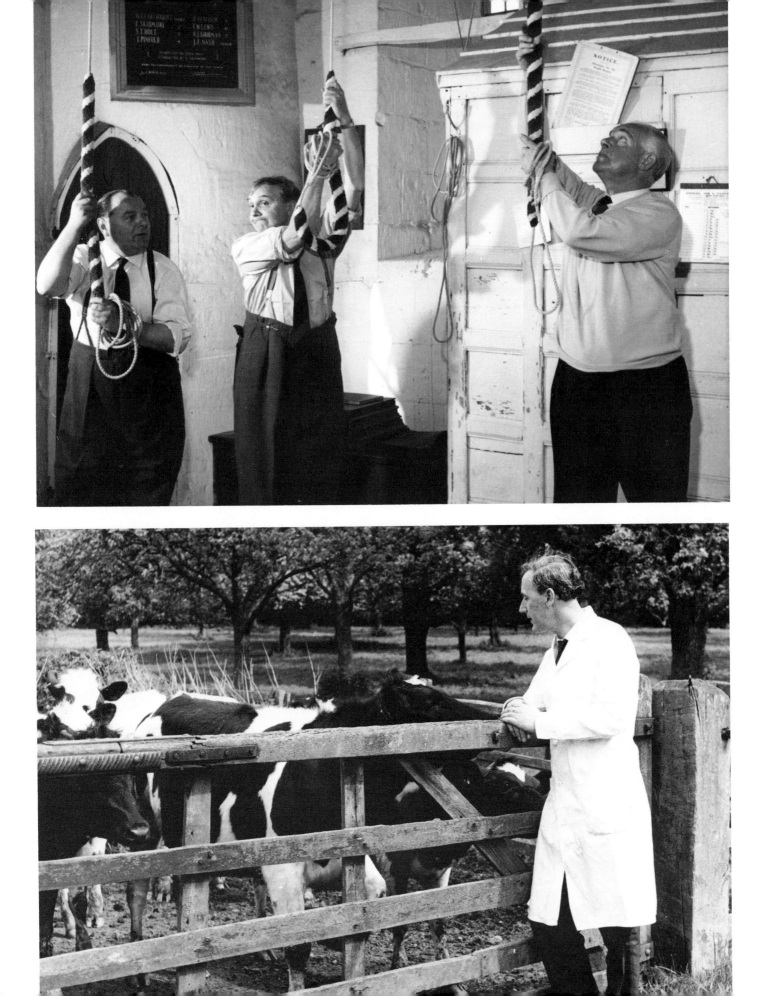

Some Ambridge Birthdays

7 January	Jennifer Aldridge		19 July	Jack Woolley
10 January	Pat Archer		27 July	Pru Forrest
14 January	Dorothy Adamson		31 July	Martha Woodford
19 January	Rachel Adamson			
21 January	Brenda Tucker		4 August	Betty Tucker
			7 August	Emma Carter
2 February	Roy Tucker		8 August	Kenton and Shula Archer
9 February	William Grundy		25 August	Walter Gabriel
15 February	Hazel Woolley		28 August	Jethro Larkin
16 February	Tony Archer		29 August	Martin Lambert
25 February	Thomas Archer			
			14 September	Rose Weston (née Larkin)
6 March	Mrs Perkins		18 September	David Archer
15 March	Richard Adamson		18 September	Joe Grundy
15 March	Eddie Grundy		23 September	Ann Tregorran
30 March	James Bellamy		28 September	Edward Grundy Jun.
			30 September	Kate Aldridge
3 April	Caroline Bone		3 October	Jill Archer
16 April	Helen Archer		10 October	Susan Carter
21 April	Elizabeth Archer		15 October	Dan Archer
23 April	Philip Archer		20 October	Tom Forrest
			24 October	George Barford
12 May	Clarrie Grundy			
15 May	Polly Perks (d. 10 Feb 1982)		1 November	Colonel Danby
22 May	Neil Carter		13 November	Peggy Archer
			13 November	Alf Grundy
			20 November	Brian Aldridge
9 June	Sid Perks			
18 June	Terry Barford		1 December	Mike Tucker
22 June	Adam Macy		7 December	Michael Adamson
			12 December	Lucy Perks
			21 December	Christine Barford
8 July	Lilian Bellamy		24 December	Deborah Macy
11 July	Doris Archer (d. 26 Oct 1980)		31 December	John Archer

The Ambridge ladies show a touch of 1960s glamour with a mannequin parade for charity. Monica Downes (Jane Rossington), Patricia Greene (Jill), Elizabeth Marlowe (Lilian), Esme Wilson (Joan Burton), June Spencer (Peggy Archer).

John Tregorran leans over Doris's shoulder to inspect the Ambridge WI produce stall in 1970.

Summer 1967, and Phil and Jill gave a christening party for their daughter Elizabeth Ann on the lawns of Hollowtree Farmhouse.

Phil and Jill enjoy dinner out at Grey Gables.

Nigel and Elizabeth, 1985

Jack May on the
bridge with Chriss
Gittins and Graham
Seed

Tom Forrest had married Pru Harris, the barmaid at The Bull, and they became foster parents to Peter Stevens and Johnny Martin. Tom grew stout with the passing years, fattened-up on Pru's puddings and pies.

Some Notable Wedding Anniversaries

1 February	John and Carol Tregorran (1967)	26 September	Tom and Pru Forrest (1958)
25 February	Neil and Susan Carter (1984)	27 September	Sid and Polly Perks (1966)
1 March	George and Christine Barford (1979)	27 September	Roger and Jennifer
11 April	Philip and Grace Archer (1955)		Travers-Macy (1968)
29 May	Brian and Jennifer Aldridge (1976)	16 November	Phil and Jill Archer (1957)
17 July	Jack and Peggy Archer (1943)	21 November	Eddie and Clarrie Grundy (1981)
3 September	Ralph and Lilian Bellamy (1971)	12 December	Tony and Pat Archer (1974)
21 September	Mark and Shula Hebden (1985)	17 December	Dan and Doris Archer (1921)

Romantic Ambridge in the 1960s: *below*: the precocious Tony Archer eavesdrops while Ambridge newcomer Sid Perks chats up Joan Hood – Philip Owen (Tony), Alan Devereux (Sid), Esme Wilson (Joan). *Opposite*: Jimmy Grange the skiffle player helps Hazel White over the stile. Alan Rothwell (Jimmy Grange), Mary Chester (Hazel White).

Opposite above: Roger Travers-Macy is tempted by the busty Jane Rossington – Jeremy Mason (Roger), Monica Downes (Jane). *Opposite below*: Nora McAuley, barmaid at The Bull, on the day of her engagement to farmworker Gregory Salt – Julia Mark (Nora), Gerald Turner (Greg).

Right: The Vicar of Ambridge, the Rev. Latimer, takes collections from church wardens Dan and Tom. Monte Cricke (Dan).

Below: Doris pours Dan a cup of coffee in the kitchen at Brookfield Farm, July 1966.

An Ambridge Calendar

January: the first Monday after Twelfth Night is 'Plough Monday', the official start of the farming year. In Penny Hassett a plough decorated with green and yellow ribbons (representing grass and corn) is drawn through the village street and money collected for charity.

February: the second of the month is Candlemas Day, when everyone hopes for bad weather:

> If Candlemas Day be fair and bright
> Winter will have another flight,
> But if Candlemas Day be wind and rain
> Winter be gone and won't come again.

On Shrove Tuesday there is a traditional pancake race in Penny Hassett.

March: the fourth Sunday in Lent is Mothering Sunday, and the Borsetshire tradition used to be for grown-up children (whether married or unmarried) to visit their mothers and eat roast pork. 25 March is Lady Day, when farm rents must be paid for the following six months.

April: there is a local tradition that anyone who gets up early on Easter morning and climbs Lakey Hill will see the sun dance. On 23 April the 'Riding of St George' takes place in Felpersham, when a man representing England's patron saint rides through the town followed by a 'dragon' (a charity float organized by the local Round Table). At some point during the month the hunting season ends.

May: May Day is celebrated with morris dancing and a maypole on the village green. Oak Apple Day on 29 May is celebrated in nearby villages by children who wear oak leaves to mark the escape of Charles II from the Parliamentarians after Worcester Fight. May is supposed to be an unhealthy month. 'A hot May makes for a fat churchyard' is a local saying. On the farm silage making is in full swing.

June: on Midsummer's Eve tradition has it that young girls can sit in the church porch at midnight and see the form of the man they will marry. On the farm, June brings sheep shearing and hay making. An old shearer's saying was:

> Here's health to the flock
> May God increase the stock
> Twenty where there's ten
> May we all come here
> Sheep shearing again.

The Ambridge church fête often takes place on the last Saturday in June, although the date is sometimes changed to fit in with fêtes held in neighbouring parishes.

July: St Swithin's Day falls on 15 July, and in the Vale of Am rain is welcomed as a help to the fruit harvest. 'St Swithin is christening the little apples' is the local saying. The poppy is in flower, and is traditionally supposed to spring from land where blood has been shed.

August: the corn harvest, known as the 'crown' of the farming year, begins in August. This month also sees the Ambridge Flower and Produce Show in the village hall.

September: The Over Sixties Club have their outing (usually to Weston-super-Mare). 29 September is Michaelmas Day, when half-yearly farm rents are paid and when farms traditionally change hands following a sale. The first Thursday after Michaelmas used to be the date of Borchester's 'mop' or 'hiring' fair, which still takes place as an entertainment with sideshows, dodgems, and hot-dog stands.

October: following the end of the corn harvest, 'cubbing' starts (it can be earlier, depending on the year). On Halloween night, according to village tradition, the images of people destined to die in the following twelve months will pass through St Stephens churchyard. The harvest festival is generally held in St Stephen's on the second Sunday of the month, followed by the harvest supper in the hall.

Carting straw at Brookfield, autumn 1966.

November: St Martin's Day is on 11 November and now passes almost unnoticed in Ambridge. In medieval times, though, it was known as 'the killing time', when most of the livestock was killed and salted against the winter. At the Martinmas Feast villagers ate their last fresh meat for many months. A favourite village saying about the weather is:

Ice before Martinmas enough to bear a duck,
The rest of the winter is sure to be but muck.

December: at nearby Edgeley Manor a yule log used to be drawn to the house on Christmas Eve, and having been lit was not supposed to have been allowed to go out during the twelve days of Christmas. In Ambridge it is believed, as elsewhere, that cattle kneel down in their stalls at midnight on Christmas Eve. The traditional meet of the South Borsetshire Hunt takes place outside the Feathers in Borchester on Boxing Day.

The Characters

DOROTHY ADAMSON is not only an unpaid assistant to her husband Richard in his pastoral duties, she also works part time in the village shop and helps to run the Playgroup. In the past she has worked as a sales assistant in a Borchester boutique and joined a gang of women roguing wild oats at Home Farm.

She and Richard have two children, Rachel and Michael, who are in their late teens.

RICHARD ADAMSON moved to the village with his family in 1973, when he became vicar of Ambridge and rector of Penny Hassett. He has since become vicar of Edgeley. Soon after he came, a new vicarage was built, and it was during a famous 'house-warming' party that Doris Archer became tiddly on Walter Gabriel's elderflower wine. Richard helps the Samaritans in Borchester, is a strong advocate of Series 3 Communion, and agreed to marry George Barford and Christine Johnson in St Stephen's Church, although George was divorced.

BRIAN ALDRIDGE appeared on the Ambridge scene in 1975 when he bought 1,500 acres of the Bellamy Estate, which was being split up after the retirement to Guernsey of Ralph and Lilian. Still only in his early thirties, his parents had been killed in a car crash, and the family farm in the Home Counties had been bought for building development, leaving him a very rich young man indeed.

A year after moving to the village he proposed to Jennifer and was accepted (Pat and Tony gave them an ironing board as a wedding present) and no expense was spared to re-convert Home Farm back from flats into a comfortable farmhouse.

1968, and Nelson had been tracked down by Interpol, tried at Gloucester Assizes, and found not guilty – and Walter could manage a wan smile as he offered young Tony Archer a drop of oil for his tractor wheel-nuts. Colin Skipp (Tony).

Educated at Sherborne, Brian has a pilot's licence and for some years was part-owner of a light plane. He has one sister, Liz, who is married to a stockbroker and lives in Cheshire.

JENNIFER ALDRIDGE is the eldest child of Peggy and Jack Archer, and Dan's first granddaughter. Born in 1945 she had a confused childhood, moving from Ambridge to Cornwall when she was six, and back again when she was seven; growing up on her father's unsuccessful smallholding, then in The Bull when her parents took over as tenants. For several weeks in 1952 she was without her mother, who was in hospital with diphtheria, and for several months in 1953 she was fatherless when Jack went into the county hospital for nervous and mental disorders.

In 1961, aged sixteen, she went on a school skiing holiday and became entangled with a ski instructor called Max (who hailed, it transpired, from Wolverhampton) and her parents were shocked to discover that she was pretending to be eighteen. In 1963 she went to the West Midland Teacher Training College at Walsall, and Jack bought her a moped. Two years later she was thrown out of her flat after a rowdy party (much to her parents' distress) and had a short story published in a magazine (much to their astonishment). It was in 1966, however, that she really made her mark, when she confessed that she was pregnant – but refused to name the father. It was only after the birth of her son, Adam, that the father was established as being Phil's dairyman Paddy Redmond, who no longer lived in Ambridge.

In 1967 she had the first of two novels published, and soon after married Roger Travers-Macy, a curious person who had appeared on the Ambridge scene calling himself Roger Patillo, and had worked as Aunt Laura's chauffeur. They moved to Borchester where Jennifer gave birth to a daughter, Deborah, but the marriage was not a success and

Jennifer eventually returned to live at Wynfords with Christine Johnson. In 1976 she married Brian Aldridge and they have a daughter, Kate.

Jennifer writes a weekly woman's page for the *Borchester Echo*, and with John Tregorran was the author of *Ambridge – A village Through The Ages* published by the Borchester Press in 1981.

MARJORIE ANTROBUS came to Ambridge in 1983 to talk to the Over Sixties about 'The Colourful World of the Afghan', and she returned in July 1984 to open the church fête. A noted dog breeder, she lived in a villa at Little Croxley, but in 1985 she bought Nightingale Farm and moved into it with Bettina and Christina and her other six breeding Afghans.

Her competitive spirit soon showed itself at the WI, where she triumphed at the monthly competition, and in the autumn she took over the editing of the parish magazine despite the horrified opposition of many villagers.

DAN ARCHER is the eldest of three sons born to John and Phoebe Archer, tenant farmers on the 100-acre Brookfield Farm, Ambridge. He was born in October 1896, and in due course went to the village school and then became a carter in the hay trade (helping at Brookfield, of course, at ploughing, sowing, and harvest). In 1916 he was called up into the 16th battalion, The Borsetshire Regiment, and spent two years procuring hay for the army in France. Then his father became seriously ill and he was discharged and sent home to look after the farm. In 1919 he was given the tenancy of Weston Farm, a forty-one acre smallholding, and in 1921 he married Doris Forrest, the daughter of a local gamekeeper. When his father died he and Doris were given the tenancy of Brookfield (his brother Ben having emigrated to Canada after fighting him for Doris, and Frank having gone to seek his fortune in New Zealand).

Dan and Doris had three children: Jack, who tried his hand at farming but eventually became landlord of the local pub after marrying Peggy Perkins of London; Christine, who is married to George Barford, the gamekeeper on the Grey Gables Estate; and Phil, who now runs Brookfield with his wife Jill and his son David.

In the Second World War Dan was chairman of the local agricultural committee, after the war he was a prominent member of the tennis club, and in his later life he was the chairman of the Parish Council. He and Doris bought Brookfield Farm in 1954 when Squire Lawson-Hope sold off the estate, and in 1970 they retired to Glebe Cottage.

Doris died of a heart attack in 1981, and Dan now lives alone – although he spends many weeks of the year at Brookfield or at The Stables with Chris and George.

DAVID ARCHER was born in September 1959 and because of his blond hair (he takes after his mother) was nicknamed 'Snowball' as a child. Always interested in farming he hoped to go to Reading University to take a degree in agriculture, but failed to get his maths 'A' level. Instead he went to the Royal Agricultural College of Cirencester for two years, and then spent almost a year on a farm in Holland.

Nowadays he is very much a manager at Brookfield, looking after the dairy side with Graham Collard and helping Phil with the paper work, as well as working flat out on a tractor or combine during ploughing and harvest.

He drives a red Triumph Spitfire which he saved up for himself (with a little help from his Mum) and girl friends have included Jackie Woodstock, Virginia Derwent, and now Sophie Barlow.

ELIZABETH ARCHER is the youngest child of Phil and Jill. Soon after she was born she was rushed into hospital and underwent a series of 'hole-in-the-heart' operations. When she was eleven she failed her exam for Borchester Grammar and was sent to boarding school where she learned the piano and flute, joined the 'Friends of the Earth', and campaigned to 'Save the Whale'. Then she became a vegetarian and took up the cello. Eventually she got eight 'O' levels (much to everybody's surprise) and went into the Sixth Form. She then became very chummy with Nigel Pargetter and in no time at all was expelled from school and came back to live at home. She is now studying Environmental Science and English Literature at Borchester Tech., still playing the cello, and takes a keen interest in the habits of barn owls.

JILL ARCHER had her blonde hair in an urchin cut and was wearing a yellow dress when Phil spied her at Ambridge Village Fête (where he was making a cine film) in 1957. A few days later he and Christine came upon her again: demonstrating something called a 'house drudge' in Underwoods. She agreed to meet him at Borchester Show, and they became friends – although she was zipping round the country (not to mention Europe) as a demonstrator. In September she got a telegram from Phil saying 'Meet me at New Street Station, Birmingham', and when they met he proposed to her and she said she'd think about it while she was in Scotland.

Later in September she came to Ambridge again, and went with Phil to a crayfish supper at The Bull. On 22 September they were having dinner at the Station Hotel, Borchester, when Phil remembered that it was the second anniversary of Grace's death, so together they took flowers to put on her grave.

On 16 November they were married, quietly, in Crudley Church, and the following year Jill gave birth to twins, who were christened Kenton and Shula. In 1959 came David, and in 1967 came Elizabeth.

Jill has been a member of the Parish Council and the Rural District Council, and has been an active supporter of the WRVS. In 1981 she was involved in running holidays for deprived children for the WRVS and in 1985 she became a local organizer. She was a member of the committee which fought to stop Borchester Grammar School going independent when Borsetshire's education system went comprehensive (Shula campaigned to make it independent) and she has been a quiet but steady opponent of bloodsports.

PAT ARCHER came to Ambridge in the summer of 1974 to look after her uncle, Haydn Evans, who had fallen and slipped a disc; and while she was tending him she met his young, go-ahead partner at Willow Farm, Tony Archer. It was only a few weeks after sports-car mad Tony had been chucked by his fiancée Mary Weston, and during harvest time that Pat (who was a decisive girl from the Welsh Valleys) proposed to him, and was accepted. They were married before the end of the year. Tony sold his sports car, and Pat bought 100 free-range hens.

On 31 December 1975 she gave birth to a son, John Daniel, and in 1979 she had a daughter, Helen, who had a dislocated hip and wore a special harness for three months. By this time the family was living at Bridge Farm, and in the autumn Pat, for the first time, showed signs of discontent with her life. She took the children to Wales without giving Tony any warning, and disappeared for two weeks. Then she returned without giving any sensible (in Tony's view) explanation and went on to puzzle him in other ways. She arbitrarily changed their newspaper from the *Daily Express* to *The Guardian*, and started to go to Women's Peace Group meetings in Borchester, leaving him at home to baby-sit. In the autumn of 1983 she brought her feminist friend Rose back to Bridge Farm and installed her in the spare room for several weeks. In 1984 she was a regular attender at Women's Studies lectures at Borchester Tech, and she became very friendly with a sociology lecturer called Roger. Then she went to a Women's Studies conference at Carmarthen with Roger, and Tony began to voice fears about the future of his marriage.

In the autumn, though, Tony resolved to 'go organic'. Pat agreed to support his efforts on the farm – and at the same time she was seen crying after a meeting with Roger in a pub. She said he was leaving Borchester.

Pat has written articles and book and film reviews and sent them to the *Borchester Echo*, but few of them have been accepted. As well as John and Helen, a third child, Tommy, was born in 1981.

PEGGY ARCHER was a stores orderly in the ATS at the end of the war, which was when she met and married Jack Archer, and came back to Ambridge with him. Her parents were Albert and Polly Perkins from the East End of London, and through her father's influence she had been brought up a non-conformist and a socialist.

In 1951 she and Jack went to live in Cornwall, where one of Jack's army pals, Barney Lee, offered them a partnership in a 120-acre farm. The following year, however, they were back – Peggy hotly pursued by an amorous Barney. She got rid of him only to succumb to diphtheria, and spent several anxious weeks in Felpersham Isolation Hospital, where she worried about rumours of a scandal involving Jack and schoolmistress Elsie Catcher.

Things settled down, and eventually she and Jack took over The Bull, and in 1959 were able to buy it when Aunt Laura gave them £4,000. Jack's fatal weakness for argument, gambling, and drink gradually got the better of him, and it was largely left to Peggy to run the pub, bring up her daughters Lilian and Jennifer and son Tony, and look after her mother, 'Mrs P', who had moved to the village soon after Peggy did back in the early 1950s.

Somewhere along the way she lost her non-conformist socialist leanings, and now lives at Blossom Hill cottage with her cat Sammy, Jack having died back in 1972.

She has been friendly for many years with Jack Woolley (although she refused his offer of marriage) and she works two days a week at the Bellamy Estate office – not because she needs the money, but to watch over the interests of her daughter Lilian.

PHIL ARCHER was born at Brookfield on St George's Day 1928, the second child of Dan and Doris, who were tenants on the 100-acre farm. He went to the village school and in 1939 won a place at Borchester Grammar, and became the first member of the Archer family to receive a full secondary education. After that he went to a Farming Institute, and by 1951 was a keen, go-ahead young farm manager earning a pound a week more than the national average. His boss was local businessman Mr Fairbrother, and he was friendly with Fairbrother's daughter, Grace. On Easter Monday 1955 he married her and they lived together in Coombe Farmhouse. That September Fairbrother offered him a directorship. He took Grace to Grey Gables to celebrate (John Tregorran, Carol Grey, and Reggie and Valerie Trentham were guests) and during the evening the stables caught fire and Grace was injured in rescuing her horse Midnight and died in Phil's arms on the way to hospital.

Two years later he had become fascinated by cine photography, and while filming the village fête (opened by Humphrey Lyttelton) he found himself filming a very attractive girl with blonde, urchin-cut hair wearing a yellow dress. Her name was Jill Patterson, and a couple of months later he proposed to her on the platform at New Street Station, Birmingham, and in November they were married quietly at Crudley Church. Phil gave up running the village cine club, and John Tregorran took it over.

During much of the 1960s Phil worked for businessman Charles Grenville then, in 1967, he joined his father and neighbouring farmer Fred Barratt to run Ambridge Dairy Farmers Ltd. Fred Barratt retired, and in 1970 so did Dan and Doris. Phil and Jill moved into Brookfield and for a time had a French au pair called Michèle Gravencin. Phil plays the piano rather well, is a local magistrate, and also serves on the PCC. He is the regular organist at St Stephen's.

SHULA MARY ARCHER is the twin daughter of Phil and Jill and was born in 1958. As a child she was passionately interested in horses, went to Ann Moore's riding school, took a horse-management course after leaving Borchester Grammar with six 'O' levels, and was determined to become a show jumper. After a year, though, she realized she would never make it to the top, so she took a job as junior clerk at Rodway and Watson's in Borchester. Since then she has taken two 'A' levels and is completing a three-year course that will give her a professional qualification as a valuer and estate agent. Blue-eyed, blonde, social secretary of Borchester Young Conservatives, her first big romance was with Simon Parker, the young, go-ahead editor of the *Borchester Echo*. After that came wealthy farmer's son Nick Wearing, who was doing a one-year practical course at Brookfield. Invited to New Zealand by a friend, Shula set off overland – and Nick went with her. A couple of months later she ran out of money in Bangkok and Phil had to send her air fare home. When she got back it emerged that she had been known as 'Lulu' in Bangkok.

In 1978 she was breathalysed and banned from driving for a year, and in 1980 she started going out with Mark Hebden, a Borchester solicitor with 'black curly hair'. On New Year's Eve he proposed and was accepted. Together they bought a cottage in Penny Hassett and acquired a kitten called Tiddles. Then Shula panicked, decided she was far too young to settle down, and called the whole thing off. Four years (and a romance with Nigel Pargetter) later she realized that she *was* ready to settle down, and at the same time Mark's engagement to Miss Sarah Locke was called off. Before she could propose to him, however, he told her he was going to

Above: Phil suffering in 1953, as the ruthless Clive Lawson-Hope attempted to steal Grace away from him; and (*below*) in 1985 as the insufferable Nigel Pargetter stole after his daughter Elizabeth. Leslie Parker (Clive Lawson-Hope), Ysanne Churchman (Grace), Graham Seed (Nigel), Alison Dowling (Elizabeth) and Norman Painting (Phil in both pictures).

In the late 1960s Jack Woolley was a confident, self-made businessman with much to be pleased about. He enjoyed the luxury of his study at Grey Gables and delighted to ramble through the winter woodlands with his adopted daughter Hazel (*bottom left*). But when walking through the market in Borchester (*bottom right*) Jack was reminded of his own grim struggle to escape from the backstreets of Birmingham. Philip Garston-Jones (Jack Wooley).

Hong Kong for a year. In the summer of 1985 she went on holiday to Hong Kong, Mark followed her back to England, and they were married in September.

TONY (ANTHONY WILLIAM DANIEL) ARCHER is the only son and youngest child of Jack and Peggy Archer. He grew up at The Bull, where his mother was the licensee (his father being weak and inclined to alcohol), and his sisters Lilian and Jennifer were bigger and stronger than he was. After leaving school he went to the Walford Farm Institute in Shropshire and then worked as a farm manager on the Bellamy estate. At this time he 'went out' with Tessa Latimer, the vicar's daughter, and almost ran away to France. After several disagreements with Bellamy he started to work for Phil at Brookfield, then in 1973 he went into partnership with Haydn Evans at Willow Farm and became engaged to farm secretary Mary Weston. Mary gave him the push after a few months, and when Haydn Evans's determined and strong-willed niece Pat proposed to him he instantly accepted. They married in December 1974. In 1978 they took over the tenancy of Bridge Farm, and in 1984 decided to go over to organic farming by abandoning artificial fertilizers.

CHRISTINE BARFORD is Dan Archer's only daughter, and was born and brought up at Brookfield with her two brothers, Jack and Phil. She went to Borchester Grammar and emerged with her HSC (distinction in biology and a credit in chemistry) to become an outside milk sampler for the Ministry of Agriculture. Early in 1954 she became involved with the squire's nephew, Clive Lawson-Hope, but she turned down his offer of marriage and he went off to Africa. She then became involved with a 'dashing horse-owner' called Paul Johnson and in February 1955 she rode a fiery mare belonging to his friend Reggie Trentham and broke her collar bone. Later, Paul invited her to go on a mysterious outing with him and Reggie, and it turned out to be a race meeting at Scowell Braddon where Paul's filly Christina was running. Paul said he wanted Christine there for luck; Dan reprimanded her for going about with racy types. A year later (after an attempted seduction by Nelson Gabriel) she married Paul, and Phil made a cine film of the event.

Although the marriage was to last for over twenty years much of it was unhappy, mainly due to Paul's business failures. Abandoning horse-training he tried his hand at running an engineering business, then a garage, then he trained as a helicopter pilot, then worked for an oil company, and finally invested everything they had in a fish farm. When that went bankrupt in 1977 he left Christine and went to Germany, where he was killed in a car crash.

Christine moved out of their home, Wynfords, and Ambridge Farmers bought the riding stables (including the indoor riding school built by Lilian) as a business for her. In March 1979 she married George Barford.

GEORGE BARFORD is a former Yorkshire policeman. He and his wife Ellen split up in 1970, and he came south to the job of assistant keeper on Lord Netherbourne's estate. In 1973 he came to Ambridge as keeper at Grey Gables, and was soon involved in a relationship with Nora, the barmaid at The Bull. She discovered that he was a reformed (just about) alcoholic, and that his wife was a Catholic and would not give him a divorce. He was distressed at being cut off from his two children, Terry and Karen. The following year he attempted suicide, and Nora moved into Lodge Cottage to look after him. She became pregnant, had a miscarriage, and in 1978 went to work in the Borchester Canning Factory where she became involved with another man. George was alone again, consoled only by his pigeon racing (in partnership with Sid Perks) and his cornet playing with the Hollerton Silver Band. Soon, though, fate began to smile on him again. His son Terry (who had been persistently delinquent as a youth) applied to join the army – and was accepted by George's old regiment from National Service days, The Prince of Wales's Own Regiment of Yorkshire. And in Ambridge he became increasingly friendly with Christine Johnson, who went with him to a Hollerton Silver Band concert and claimed she liked his uniform of bottle green with magenta stripes. His wife Ellen then gave him a divorce, and in November Christine agreed to marry him. Members of the Hollerton Silver Band formed a triumphal archway with bugles outside the church; Tom Forrest was his best man; and Jennifer laid on a wedding reception at Home Farm.

In the 1960s Ralph Bellamy was the 'Squire' of Ambridge and was casting a thoughtful but sad eye on young Lilian Archer – who was about to marry Canadian air force pilot Lester Nicholson. Jack Holloway (Ralph Bellamy).

In December 1984 Terry (now a corporal in the Prince of Wales's Own) was seriously hurt in a road accident in Berlin, and George was flown out to his bedside by the Army.

DAVID BARRY is a detective-sergeant with the Borsetshire Constabulary, stationed at Borchester police station. In 1982 he arrested Nelson Gabriel on suspicion of handling stolen goods, but had to let him go. In the same year he nearly arrested Eddie Grundy for rustling cattle from Home Farm, but eventually concluded that he was innocent.

In 1983 he became closely involved with Ambridge life when he investigated the disappearance of the Over Sixties' tea money, and soon after he bought the old police house and had a flirtation with Hazel Woolley. Then, in 1984, he became friendly with Kathy Holland, Lucy Perks's school teacher. He changed a wheel on her car, and she invited him

to tea, then they went together to the police social. When Kathy was distressed by the reappearance of her husband he helped her through the crisis, and she gave him lots of advice about redecorating his new house.

LILIAN BELLAMY is the younger daughter of Jack and Peggy Archer; her sister is Jennifer, married to Brian Aldridge of Home Farm; and her brother is Tony Archer of Bridge Farm.

Born in 1947 Lilian grew up on her parents' smallholding, then at The Bull. After finishing school she went to a riding academy near Felpersham and qualified as a riding instructor in 1967. A year later she met and married a Canadian airforce pilot called Lester Nicholson, who died in a Canadian hospital in 1970. Her second husband was the village 'squire', Ralph Bellamy, a man considerably older than herself who died from a heart attack at their Guernsey home in 1979.

Lilian still lives on Guernsey. She has one son, James, by her second marriage. Although she rarely visits Ambridge she has considerable influence in the area, being the landlord of her brother Tony at Bridge Farm, the Grundys at Grange Farm, and the Tuckers at Ambridge Farm. She has also had financial dealings with Nelson Gabriel.

CAROLINE BONE belongs to the ancient Bone (or Bohun) family of Darrington Manor; her ancestors were in the breach at Agincourt and on the beaches at Dunkirk; she is distantly related to Lord Netherbourne (she has always called him 'Uncle') and to the Duke of Westminster; and her younger brother Tim is a lieutenant in a crack cavalry regiment, the Queen's Own Hussars.

Caroline went to boarding school, then did a two-year cookery and hotel management course based in Lausanne and Paris. She first came to Ambridge in 1977 (together with a very large dog called Leo) and worked as a temporary live-in barmaid for Sid and Polly at The Bull. Then she went to Bristol to open a wine bar with some friends. The venture proved unsuccessful, and Sid asked her back to transform the food being served in The Bull. Her attempts to introduce *cordon bleu* cookery met with mixed success (locals persisted in stubbornly demanding steak-and-onion pies and sausages), and in

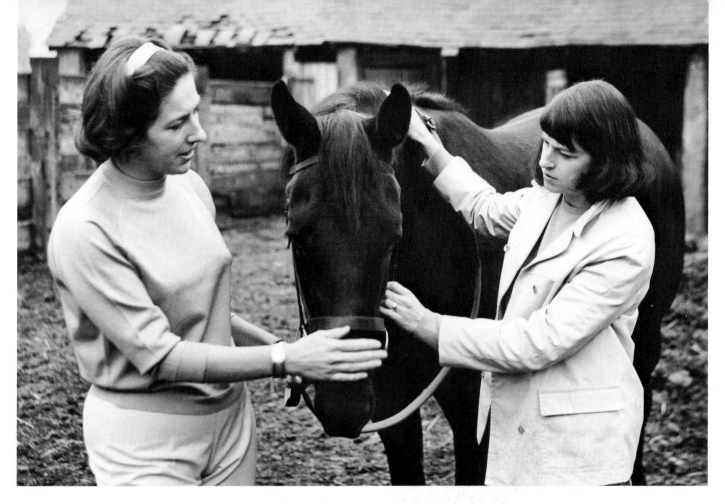

Christine Johnson inspects a horse at Brookfield with Lilian, soon after her marriage to Nick. A few months later he would be dead – and a year after that, in 1971, she would marry Ralph. Elizabeth Marlowe (Lilian).

early 1980 she moved to Grey Gables as Jack Woolley's personal assistant. Since then she has looked after shooting parties in winter and riding holidays in summer, and has introduced *nouvelle cuisine* to the restaurant.

She has not been fortunate in affairs of the heart: a romance with former SAS officer Alan Frazer came to nothing; her friendship with a sea-harrier pilot, Paul Chubb, ended when he decided to marry somebody else; and a sad, secret relationship with Brian Aldridge got her nowhere at all.

NEIL CARTER came to Brookfield as a sixteen-year-old 'new entrant' farming apprentice in 1973. He lodged with Martha Woodford who looked after him and mothered him, then he met a girl called Sandy Miller in Borchester, and she invited him to a party, and the police raided it and discovered 'reefers' in his pocket. The drugs had been planted

on him by Sandy, but he nobly refused to implicate her in court. Placed on probation he also painted Walter Gabriel's porch as part of a community service order.

In 1976 he left Martha Woodford and moved into a flat at Nightingale Farm. Shula cooked a meal and played her guitar for him one evening, and for a few brief, delirious days he wondered if he was going to marry the boss's daughter. He bought green wellington boots and a new anorak, and drove his tractor into a gatepost because he was waving and grinning at her. When, however, Shula told him they could only be 'good friends' he took the news with fortitude. After a succession of girl friends (one of them, Vikki, turned out to be an animals' rights protester) he became engaged to a bright Brummie barmaid from The Bull, Julie, who moved into Nightingale Farm with him. In 1983, though, she moved out again and went in search of the bright lights. At the village fête that year Susan Horobin won a pig and Neil gave her some food for it and offered to build her a pig pen, and a week or two later Susan invited him out for a meal in Borchester.

They were married in 1984, and Susan gave birth

to a baby girl, Emma. At the end of the year they moved out of Nightingale Farm (the owner, Hugo Barnaby, offered them £4,000 if they would enable him to sell the property with vacant possession) and now live in one of the council houses facing the village green. Neil has a small business of his own – battery hens and deep-litter birds – which he keeps in sheds at Willow Farm.

SUSAN CARTER used to be Susan Horobin before her marriage, and grew up in a council house on The Green with her terrible brothers Keith, Stuart, and Gary, and her poor little sister Tracy. In 1983 she started working full time behind the bar in The Bull, and Tom Forrest described her as 'nice and fresh-looking, not a bit like the other Horobins',

Evensong at St Stephen's, 1969. Dan Archer holds out the collection plate for Greg Salt's half-crown. In the front row is bearded John Tregorran – finally married to Carol, who is singing along next to him. Edgar Harrison (Dan Archer), Philip Morant (John Tregorran).

but Clarrie Grundy described her as 'sly, with short stumpy legs' because she thought Eddie and Susan were getting too friendly.

At the church fête that year Susan won a pig (called Pinky) and Neil Carter helped her to feed it, and to catch it when her brothers let it out of its sty, and he made Eddie give her a fair price when she was forced to sell it. At Christmas he was protective when her brothers made her ill by playing *The Texas Chainsaw Massacre* over and over on the video, and took her for a short-break holiday in London where she told him that she was pregnant.

They were married in 1984 and in due course Susan gave birth to a little girl, Emma Louise, who gave them a few worrying moments when she developed jaundice.

LIEUTENANT COLONEL FREDERICK DANBY retired from the army in 1976 and became the Borsetshire and Gloucestershire area representative for a national charity. He first came to Am-

bridge when he answered Laura Archer's advert for a paying guest at Ambridge Hall.

Since then he has become a prominent member of the village community, and is the chairman of the Parish Council. He is warmly respected by the Archer family for the way he looked after Laura in the weeks before her death in February 1985.

'Freddie', as he is known, did not retire from the army a rich man, and helping with the upkeep of Ambridge Hall was a severe strain on his pension. In recent years he has sold damsons from a roadside stall, been a forecourt attendant at Wharton's Garage, and been the hunt correspondent.

He and Laura dabbled in self-sufficiency, and cared for a succession of animals that included Edric the Pig (eaten by Freddie and Laura), Heidi the Goat (eaten by a passing lynx), Jessica the Hen (rescued from a battery house) and numerous ducks including Rebecca, Jemima, and Mr Drake that lived in a hut called Duckingham Palace.

In the spring of 1985 Laura's great niece Judy Cameron was traced in New Zealand and inherited Laura's estate (it should have gone to Freddie, but Laura didn't sign her will) Miss Cameron was happy for Freddie to stay on as her 'tenant' at Ambridge Hall.

PRU FORREST was thirty years old when she became friendly with the vigorous gamekeeper from the Squire's estate, Tom Forrest, back in 1956. Her name was Prudence Harris in those days, and she lived at home with her mother. Soon afterwards Bob Larkin started to pester her, and Tom threatened to bash his face in – then Tom killed Bob when he was out one night prowling after poachers.

Pru supported Tom during the subsequent manslaughter trial, and they were married in 1958. Unable to have children of their own they fostered two boys, Johnnie Martin and Peter Stephens. In 1972 she was very upset when Sid and Polly 'sacked' her from working at The Bull (they couldn't afford her wages) and for several days insisted that Tom shouldn't drink there.

In 1976 she and Tom worked together at the new Garden Centre at Grey Gables, but the following year Jack Woolley was forced to bring in an expert manager. Pru retired, although Tom kept on as a part-time gamekeeper on the estate.

Nowadays Pru is famed for her sloe gin, her blackcurrant cheesecake, and for winning an impressive number of prizes at the annual Flower and Vegetable Show.

TOM FORREST still works part time as a gamekeeper for Jack Woolley – doing the same work in the same woods that he has done ever since he left Ambridge village school back in 1924. His father was a gamekeeper before him, working for Squire Lawson-Hope, and his elder sister Doris married Dan Archer of Brookfield Farm. Tom led a quiet bachelor life until his forties, when he found himself becoming attached to young Pru Harris, the barmaid at The Bull, and while he was slowly thinking about courting her, Ned Larkin's brother Bob came on the scene and became attached to her himself. A week or two later Tom shot and killed Bob Larkin one night while out searching for poachers. He was arrested and charged with manslaughter. In due course he was tried at Gloucester Assizes, found not guilty, and returned to Ambridge in triumph, accompanied by the Borchester Silver Band. He married Pru Harris (after a deal of agonizing) and soon afterwards she was given a routine X-ray and found to have a patch on her lung. She was sent to a sanatorium for several weeks.

Tom and Pru were unable to have children, but they did foster two boys, Johnnie Martin and Peter Stephens, and Peter still lives in the area (he is married and works as a garage mechanic in Borchester) and keeps in touch.

Tom has had many a brush with poachers in his time, and there have been other excitements in his rustic life. In 1974 he found George Barford semiconscious after taking an overdose of sleeping pills, and the same year he helped to catch thieves who were using a furniture van in broad daylight to rob the Dower House.

When he first went into semi-retirement Tom and Pru ran the new Garden Centre at Grey Gables; but they were not happy, and Tom went back to keepering.

NELSON GABRIEL did his National Service in the RAF where he was promoted to corporal, then sergeant, and decided to stay on in the service of her Majesty for a further five years. He came home to

Walter Gabriel still had yearnings to be a farmer, but by 1970 he was looking very confused when Dan gave him advice about sending fat lambs to market.

Ambridge at irregular intervals, bearing gifts of nylon stockings for the girls (including Christine Archer) and in 1953 was taken seriously ill and sent to an RAF hospital in Southampton. His father Walter was rushed to his bedside and required to give many pints of blood. After his recovery Nelson went off to a new posting somewhere in the Med.

In the early 1960s he was out of the RAF and moved to Borchester, from where he sent his dad £10 and said he was going to marry a rich businessman's daughter. Nothing came of it, and in 1966 he started going out with young Jennifer Archer from The Bull (when she became pregnant Nelson was the prime suspect). He also opened a casino in Borchester in partnership with Toby Stobeman, and fleeced Jennifer's father, Jack, of all his money.

In May 1967 he was reported dead after his light plane crashed over the coast of France. A couple of months later, however, his fingerprints were discovered on an empty scotch bottle in the hideout of the Borchester Mail Van robbers, and it was decided that he was not dead after all. In 1968 he was tracked down by Interpol (he had parachuted out of the plane before it crashed) and brought back to England to stand trial for armed robbery. Members of the gang testified that he had been known by them as 'the Boss'. Despite the evidence he was acquitted, to the delight of his poor father who had known he was innocent all along. In 1970 he emerged as the owner of a block of flats at Hollowtree, offered Jack Archer's other daughter Lilian the chance to live in one of them rent free, and then attempted to make passionate love to her in it. Soon after he left Ambridge and became a property speculator in London and Spain.

Little was heard of his movements until 1979, when he reappeared in the village just before Christmas, bounced a cheque in The Bull and was unable to pay his bill at Grey Gables. He spent the festive season miserably with his father in Honeysuckle

Cottage. A year later he again came back to Borset-shire, but this time with enough money to run an old Jaguar and rent premises in Borchester which he turned into a wine bar. Since then he has bought the freehold, opened an antique shop next to it (join-ing the two premises together), and been suspi-ciously involved with an antique dealers' 'ring'. In 1984 he again ran into serious debt after engaging a singer from the Ritz called Hebe to appear in his newly-styled 'cocktail' bar, and again disappeared to London for several weeks. He reappeared after hav-ing sold out the final asset from his golden days as a Man of the World – a part-share in a garage and flat in Lanzarotte.

WALTER GABRIEL is the oldest inhabitant of the village (he's two months older than Dan, even) and was made a widower in the 1930s when his wife

Some very doubtful looks at the Brookfield straw harvest from Tony, Phil, and Dan.

Annie died, leaving him to bring up their only child, Nelson. For many years Walter struggled as a tenant farmer, but in 1957 he gave up his smallholding and turned to other activities, including a partnership in the Hollerton Pet Shop with Agatha Turvey, a pig venture, and a maggot-breeding business. He ran a junk stall for some time, and had a stuffed gorilla called George. In 1964 he played Long John Silver (with a real parrot) in the vicar's pantomime, and in 1965 he bought an elephant called Rosie who had a baby called Tiny Tim. He also ran a bus service and a short-stay caravan site.

In 1966 he found forty-two gold sovereigns hid-den up a chimney, and fifteen years later wads of pound notes stuffed inside an easy chair. He bought a boat, once, with Jack Archer, and they kept it on the River Severn. Thugs attacked and injured him in the village shop, and other thugs tried to ambush the postbus when he was riding in it, causing him to lose his false teeth while escaping over the fields. He had a nasty moment in 1967 when a certain

Sid Perks with a sack of carrots outside the Ambridge stores.
Alan Devereux (Sid).

Nancy Tarrant turned up on his doorstep claiming
to be pregnant by Nelson (he sent her away and
promised her money), a horrible time in 1977 when
the roof of Honeysuckle Cottage had to be replaced
and he was homeless for several months, and a
poorly time in 1979 when he was taken to hospital
with a sugar imbalance and nobody could track
down Nelson. In recent years, though, Nelson has
been dutiful in tending his garden, Mrs P ever so-

licitous about his welfare, Jill Archer has brought
him his meals-on-wheels, and Martin Lambert the
vet has given him a budgerigar called Joey.

CLARRIE GRUNDY was born in Dorset, and
came to Ambridge in 1966 when her father Jethro
Larkin got a job as general worker at Brookfield
Farm. When she was seventeen she was described
as 'jolly and fat' and she got a job working in the
kitchen at The Bull. Her dream, though, was to
become an airline hostess, and in pursuit of this she
got herself a job as office girl at a Borchester travel

agent's. When that job folded she worked as a daily help at Brookfield, then at Borchester Dairies bottling plant, then as permanent barmaid in The Bull.

In 1980 a new kitchen range was installed at Woodbine Cottage and Eddie Grundy was employed to remove the old one, and after a day or two of chatting-up he asked her out for a chop-suey in Borchester's Woo-Ping restaurant. Following this Clarrie hoped for an early engagement, but Eddie was determined to be a free spirit. Over a year later Clarrie heard about the engagement of Lady Diana Spencer to the Prince of Wales and cried as she sang 'One Day My Prince Will Come'.

Then her mother, Lizzie, died, and she got £500 insurance money, and Eddie became suddenly more attentive – he needed cash to pay for a demo record – and Clarrie wisely withheld her money until Eddie agreed that some of it should be spent on a white gold engagement ring with a single ruby.

She walked out on her father when he refused to give her away, but he relented, and on 21 November 1981 she and Eddie were married in Ambridge Church. Eddie wore a brown suit with maroon shoes, and one of the hymns was 'All things bright and beautiful'.

Clarrie's life since then has not been easy. She has struggled to make a garden at Grange Farm, and seen piles of scrap metal dumped on it. In 1982 she fell downstairs and nearly had a miscarriage after Eddie had walked out on her. She does, though, have two strong sons to be proud of, William and Edward, and she regards herself as unbelievably lucky to be married to a Country and Western singing star.

EDDIE GRUNDY was born on 15 March 1951, the younger son of Joe and Susan Grundy, tenant farmers of Grange Farm, Ambridge. He went to the village school and then to Borchester Secondary Modern, during which time he used to kiss and cuddle Lilian Bellamy (he is fond of remembering) in the back of the school bus.

In 1977 he was courting a scrap-merchant's daughter, and in 1979 he became engaged to divorcee Dolly Treadgold. His father decorated the Grange Farm Turkey Shed with bunting for the wedding reception, but Eddie called the whole thing off because Dolly was 'too flighty'. After that he had

Having a drink with Sid in 1971 is Tony Archer – who had a complicated year ahead of him. His girlfriend Jane Petrie was to give him the push, Bellamy was to sack him, and he was to run away to France without telling anybody.

a couple of wild years in which he tried to seduce Eva the au pair, was hit over the head in The Bull and banned from drinking there, and was accused of stealing materials from his employers, Hollerton Plant Hire. In 1980 he became friendly with Clarrie Larkin and took her down into his 'saloon cellar' at Grange Farm to listen to his stereo and admire the bison he had painted on the wall. Later in the year he sang 'The Cowboy's Farewell to his Horse' at the vicar's 'Songs of Praise' in Ambridge Church.

In 1981 he made his own record 'Lambs to the Slaughter' with Jolene Rogers, the Lily of Leyton Cross, and disappeared to do a series of 'gigs' with her in London. He returned home penniless – Jolene had run off with Wayne Tucson, the singing oilman from Hollerton, and taken his share of the record money.

In November he was married to Clarrie, the girl who had stood by him during his troubles and given him her Mum's insurance money. They live at Grange Farm with their sons William and Edward, and Eddie does the work of the farm virtually single-handed.

He still dreams of being a Country and Western singing star, and has made two further records with the Borchester C and W Club: 'Poor Pig' and 'Clarrie'. In 1983 he was again banned from The Bull after being sick in a piano.

JOE GRUNDY is the eldest and only surviving son of George Grundy, who was given the tenancy of Grange Farm when he came back from Palestine in 1919 and became a famous cricketer in the Borsetshire Minor League. Joe took over the tenancy in the early 1950s and farmed with his wife Susan and their two sons Alfred and Edward. Susan died in

1969, and in the following year both Joe's dairy herd and his sons contracted brucellosis. In 1971 he was given notice to quit by Ralph Bellamy. He survived, however, and in 1973 was co-opted on to the Parish Council in the place of Mrs Tonks. In 1976 he had the good fortune to win a luxury weekend at Grey Gables (he turned up alone, and demanded half the prize in cash) but a year later he was unlucky enough to be hit over the head by Terry Barford when he was out earth-stopping for the hunt.

In 1978 Alf left the farm to go scrap-metal dealing in Gloucester, and Eddie disappeared off with a blowsy blonde from the Borchester bus station cafeteria leaving his father delirious with flu. Then half the herd went down with brucellosis and Joe's favourite hob ferret Turk was found dead in a trap. For several weeks he seemed to give up the will to fight against the trials and tribulations of life, but then Eddie returned and he recovered his spirits. In 1982 he received a severe shock when Eddie's wife Clarrie gave a gallon of his best Kingston Black Cider to the vicar for a tombola stall, and he spent a small fortune trying to win it back. The following

Tom Forrest inspecting the fruit trees with his wife Pru. Mary Dalley (Pru Forrest).

year he was banned from The Bull after Eddie had been sick in Sid Perks's piano. Then he became attached to Martha Woodford – 'a nice little widow-woman with a pound or two in the bank and a dab hand at making puddings' – and built her a bird table. Martha, however, preferred the attentions of retired farmer Bill Insley. In 1984 the Grange Farm combine caught fire, and at Lady Day 1985 Joe had difficulty raising his half-yearly rent. He was consoled, though, by pleasant afternoons watching 'Playschool' with grandson William, and bingo sessions in the village hall with the Over Sixties. He has written two 'chapters' of an autobiography called *A Straight Furrow, by Joe Grundy, 'Man of the Land'* which is designed to expose the way his father George was cheated out of the Brookfield tenancy while he was away fighting in the First World War.

Shula dreamed of being a show-jumper, but when she was sixteen her father insisted that she first take a secretarial course at Borchester tech. When she did, she became unfortunately involved with a hi-fi enthusiast called Eric. Judy Bennett (Shula).

MARK HEBDEN went to Shrewsbury School, read Law at Durham University, and qualified as a solicitor in 1977. His parents live in Borchester (his mother, Bunty, is a flower-arranger and golfer of renown) and he returned home, joined the Round Table (his father is a Rotarian of note) and got a job as assistant solicitor with a local firm. Two years later he met Shula (who was taken by his curly black hair) and she took him home to Brookfield and he helped Phil with the hay harvest. In the following months he was kicked and badly hurt by a dying deer while he was pursuing poachers in the Country Park, and took Shula up in a hot-air balloon to celebrate her birthday. He quarrelled with Shula over a legal case involving hunt saboteurs, but she forgave him on New Year's Eve when he proposed marriage. 'Yes', she said, and they bought a cottage together in Penny Hassett, and did it up together, and acquired a cat called Tiddles. In the summer of 1981, though, with the marriage only days away, Shula panicked and changed her mind. The wedding was called off.

In the following two years Mark had a long affair

with Jackie Woodstock (Nelson's assistant at the Wine Bar), inherited £25,000, considered becoming a blacksmith, and was engaged to solicitor's daughter Sarah Locke.

In 1984 he defended Shula when she was jointly charged with taking and driving away. His forthcoming marriage to Sarah Locke was called off. After Shula's acquittal he announced that he was going to Hong Kong for a year (Shula hoped they might be able to announce something quite different) and he left on 1 September. He returned and married her in September 1985.

KATHY HOLLAND teaches home economics at Borchester Grammar School, where she was Lucy Perks's form mistress for a year, and she also rents the Perks's cottage in Penny Hassett. She is married

True romance blossomed for Tony Archer in 1974. He had been jilted by his fiancée Mary Weston, but at harvest time Pat Lewis came to the village and proposed to him, and he accepted happily. Patricia Gallimore (Pat).

but separated from her husband. In 1984 he came to Borchester and tried to persuade her to give their marriage 'another chance', but she turned him down. She seemed to be very close to Sid Perks at one time, but in the crisis with her husband she turned to Detective Sergeant Barry for support, and they became steady friends in the spring and summer of 1985.

BILL INSLEY came to Ambridge in 1983, after selling his 300-acre farm near Ashbourne in Derbyshire. He is a widower with two grown-up daughters, and since buying Willow Farmhouse he has become interested in rare breeds of pig – Gloucester Old Spots and Large Blacks. He bought a Large Black boar called Eros in the spring of 1984. At around the same time he seemed to be courting Martha Woodford, and took her on a bank holiday outing to a pig farm. Then he lost interest (in Martha, not the pigs) and started to encourage Neil Carter in his egg business. He allowed Neil to use

one of the Willow Farm outbuildings for his battery hens, and another for his deep-litter birds.

MARTIN LAMBERT is a thirty-year-old assistant vet at Bill Robertson's practice in Borchester. He previously worked for two years in Somerset. Martin has responsibility for routine herd visits in the Ambridge area. In October 1984 he bumped into Shula Archer at Borchester Fair, and started to take her out on a fairly regular basis. He also made himself popular in Ambridge by giving Walter Gabriel a budgie called Joey, and throwing Eddie Grundy in the River Am on Bonfire Night. In 1985 he told Shula that their friendship must either become closer or must end. She ended it.

JETHRO LARKIN is the son of Ned and Mabel Larkin, who lived in the village for many years and were famous local characters. Ned Larkin worked at Brookfield Farm, and Mabel was a cleaning lady of great fame. In his youth Jethro left Ambridge to see the world, and got as far as Dorset where he settled down as a farm worker. In 1966 he returned, bringing with him a wife, Lizzie, and two apple-cheeked daughters, Rosie and Clarrie.

His life has not been without incident and excitement: in 1975 he broke a leg while loading baled hay at Brookfield, and in 1978 his Uncle Charlie died and left him over £4,000. Rosie married a chap called Dennis and moved to Great Yarmouth, and Clarrie married Eddie Grundy and moved to Grange Farm. In September 1980 Jethro's wife Lizzie died of a stroke, and he now lives alone (except for his dog Gyp) in Woodbine Cottage.

NIGEL PARGETTER attended the opening meet of the South Borset Hunt on 5 November 1983 and fell off his horse in Phil's barley. On 15 November he burst into the kitchen at Brookfield wear-

A mid-morning cup of coffee makes a welcome break for Phil and Jill during the Brookfield harvest, 1975.

Aunt Laura on the warpath, as she organized the Ambridge Protection Society to stop the village's last surviving elm tree from being chopped down. Betty McDowell (Aunt Laura).

ing his gorilla suit, after terrifying Tom Forrest by going 'Unga unga!' at him in the Country Park. Three weeks later he organized a party at Grey Gables to celebrate almost selling a swimming pool to Jack Woolley, and he and Shula mixed cocktails in Jack's Chrysanthemum Society Challenge Cup and did the Conga through the bedroom-wing carrying a stag's head.

Nigel is the only son (though he has a younger sister) of Gerald and Julia Pargetter of Lower Loxley House, Loxley Barratt (generally referred to as Pargetter Hall), and in his day was a leading light (with Tim Beecham and Shula Archer) of Borchester Young Conservatives. In April 1984, when he had taken Shula to the Hunt Ball and was sup-

posedly sleeping on the sofa at Brookfield he upped and crept into Phil and Jill's bedroom whispering 'cuckoo' and 'tally-ho!' and jumped into bed on Phil's side. He claimed he was looking for the bathroom but was banned from Brookfield for some time. Later in 1984 he 'borrowed' a sports car he thought belonged to Tim Beecham (it didn't) and was convicted of taking and driving away. Shula gave him the push and he started going out with Elizabeth. He got sacked from selling swimming pools and Elizabeth chucked him. His family held a conference and sent him to an uncle in Zimbabwe. After a few weeks he returned and gave everyone little wooden elephants.

Nigel has pet mice which he races in the Pargetter racing colours.

In the summer of 1985, he was 'Mr Snowy' and drove an ice-cream van. In the Autumn he sold toffee-apples at Borchester Fair.

MRS PERKINS is the mother of Peggy Archer, and she came to Ambridge when she was widowed, in 1951, and lodged for some time at the cottage of an asthmatic Londoner called Bill Slater who was eventually killed in a brawl outside The Bull. In those days Mrs Perkins (known in the Archer family as 'Mrs P') was described as a 'sharp-featured, black-coated woman with a deal of furniture'. For several decades she has been amorously pursued by Walter Gabriel (these days more as a matter of form than conviction) and she lives in one of the Old Folk's bungalows in Manorfield Close, next door to Mrs Bagshawe and not far from Mrs Potter.

SID PERKS was a callow teenager with a record of trouble with the police when he came to Ambridge in 1963, but Jack Woolley had sympathy for him (two working-class Brummie lads together) and gave him a job as his chauffeur. The following year Sid took pretty Polly Mead, the barmaid from The Bull, to Hollerton Fair, and his motor-bike was stolen by louts who knew him from his unsavoury former life. Sid became engaged to Polly, but the romance was broken-off when she left The Bull to work at the Regency Hotel in Borchester. In 1966, though, she turned to him for comfort when her father was exposed as a pyromaniac, and they were married in September. Jack Woolley arranged their

In 1976 Ambridge newcomer Brian Aldridge proposed to Jennifer Travers-Macy, and they were married as soon as her divorce came through. Brian bought her twelve Jacob sheep, and she washed them regularly and took up spinning and weaving. Angela Piper (Jennifer).

honeymoon in Cornwall and provided them with a car to get there.

In 1967 Sid stopped working for Woolley and had a difficult couple of years. He was employed for a while by Phil Archer at the Hollowtree Pig Unit, then worked for a mysterious Mr Brown. It turned out that Mr Brown's pig unit was a 'front' for a gang of professional gamblers, and the job fell through. Sid then worked for Paul Johnson as a mechanic at the village garage.

By 1969, however, Sid and Polly were installed running the village shop (which they turned into a self-service store) and in 1971 their daughter Lucy was born. A year later they left the shop and moved to The Bull, working for the owner, Peggy Archer. Because of Sid's previous criminal record it was Polly who became the licensee. In 1976 they bought a cottage in Penny Hassett (Rose Cottage) as an investment for their future, and spent months and months renovating it. Sid also started a hobby – keeping and racing pigeons in partnership with George Barford.

In 1982 Polly was killed in a road accident, and Sid faced the problem of bringing Lucy up on his own. In 1984 he became friendly with one of Lucy's teachers, Kathy Holland, who was also the tenant of Rose Cottage.

MARY POUND now lives in a bungalow at Edgeley, but for many years she and her husband Ken were the tenants at Ambridge Farm, and ran a farm shop during the summer months. Their daughter Marilyn is married to Harry Booker, the postman. Ken Pound died in 1983 after a long illness.

CAROL TREGORRAN still runs the market garden she started in 1954 when she came to Ambridge from Surrey, and bought a smallholding off Dan Archer. In those days she was called Carol Grey, and was described as a 'good-looking young woman, extremely well dressed', and she caused a stir when it was discovered that she ran her own car. Soon after her arrival she was driving past Coombe Farm when she knocked John Tregorran off his scooter. He proposed to her at a party and she refused him (as, indeed, she was to do many times over the next decade or so). John then took her to look at a rare wild flower in the woods and she was bitten on the wrist by an adder.

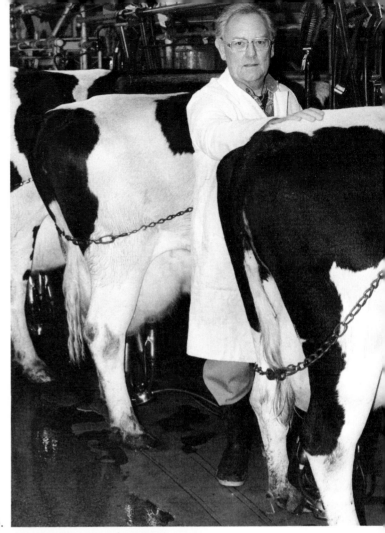

Right: Phil in the milking parlour at Brookfield, on Graham Collard's day-off.

Eddie Grundy is unaffected by his father's biting sarcasm. In 1979 Eddie was engaged to Dolly Treadgold, and Joe decorated the turkey-shed for a reception and ordered sandwiches and lots of little vol-au-vents from The Bull. Then Eddie jilted Dolly because she was too fickle, and a month or two later started to impress barmaid Clarrie Larkin with his smooth-singing ways. Trevor Harrison (Eddie), Haydn Jones (Joe).

In 1958 she had another nasty experience when a boat she was in was reported missing in heavy seas, but she returned safely and became friendly with Charles Grenville, a hard-headed domineering businessman who had bought the Manor. Their friendship cooled because Carol disliked Grenville's housekeeper, Madame Garonne, but when M. Garonne disappeared and was revealed by the *Borchester Echo* as a diamond smuggler, Grenville apologized, and the friendship was resumed. They went on a business trip to Holland with Phil Archer, and when Phil was taken into hospital Grenville proposed to Carol and was accepted.

In 1963 Grenville was badly injured in a car crash (John Tregorran's wife Janet was killed in the same accident) and in 1965 he died in America (a mystery bug, picked up years before in the East). In 1966 John Tregorran again proposed, and was accepted, and they were married on 1 February 1967.

In 1975 Carol had a bad time when she was accused of shoplifting in Felpersham, and fought the

The Grundy Wedding Album: *Right*: The happy couple in the porch at St Stephen's. *Below*: the wedding reception at The Bull. Almost impaled on Eddie's cowhorn hat is the errant Nelson Gabriel, now returned to Borchester's cafe society. Heather Bell (Clarrie), Jack May (Nelson).

Left: Doris arranges the flowers in St Stephen's. In 1981 she died after a heart attack which happened while she was resting quietly at home in Glebe Cottage. A year later there was another death in the village when Polly Perks (*above*) was killed in a road accident. Hilary Newcombe (Polly).

Sid Perks comforts daughter Lucy, after the death of Polly in 1982. Alan Devereux (Sid), Tracy Jane-White (Lucy).

case to the Crown Court before being acquitted. In 1980 she behaved discreetly and well when John became romantically attached to Jennifer Aldridge for a short time.

JOHN TREGORRAN appeared on the Ambridge scene as a 'bearded young wanderer with a green caravan' in 1953, but was soon revealed as a university lecturer who had won £12,000 on the football pools. Walter Gabriel allowed him to put the caravan in his rickyard and a few days later it was damaged when gypsies set fire to it. A few months later the gypsies attacked John and beat him up (he had taken too close an interest in their affairs, and in one of their womenfolk).

In 1954 he proposed marriage to Carol Grey, but she turned him down. Over the years he asked her again and again, but to no avail. He opened an antiques shop in Borchester, took over running the Ambridge Cine Club from Phil, and played Father Christmas at the Ambridge Fayre, but he was unable to get Carol out of his mind. In 1959 she was late for a date with him at the Bear Hotel in Bor-

A fond look for gamekeeper George Barford from his new wife Christine, as they depart for their honeymoon. Graham Roberts (George Barford), Lesley Saweard (Chris).

chester, and she found him half-drunk because of his misery. The next year she married Charles Grenville, a rich businessman who had come to live in Ambridge.

John remained friends with them both, and in 1963 married pretty blue-eyed district nurse Janet Sheldon. In October Janet and Charles were in a car together when it crashed. Janet was killed, Charles badly injured. The following year Charles went to America on business and decided to stay there. Soon after he collapsed and died. John, meanwhile, had gone to Spain where he had spent several weeks in hospital after problems with his vocal cords. He returned to England and opened a bookshop in Borchester, and took a prominent part in organizing the Ambridge Summer Festival, which featured the Garden of Eden with Walter Gabriel's elephants Rosie and Tiny Tim. He proposed to Carol yet again – and this time was accepted, and they were married, and bought Manor Court for £20,000. Apart from a brief romance (mainly on John's part) with Jennifer Aldridge in 1981 they have lived happily ever since. John spends a large part of his time travelling and lecturing on antique furniture.

BETTY TUCKER was born in 1950 and came to Ambridge in 1973 when her husband Mike became dairy manager at Brookfield. They lived in Rickyard Cottage for several years, and Betty kept bees and goats, and they had a go at breeding pedigree sheep dogs. In 1978 she gave birth to a son, Roy, and in 1981 a girl, Brenda. By this time the family had moved to Willow Farm, where Mike had a partnership agreement with Haydn Evans, and where Betty ran a lively bed-and-breakfast business. In 1983 they were given the tenancy of Ambridge Farm and

In 1980 Shula found a new boyfriend, twenty-six-year-old Mark Hebden, a Borchester solicitor, and by the end of the year they had got engaged. Richard Derrington (Mark).

Betty tried to run a farm shop but could not cope with the extra work involved.

Betty helps Dorothy Adamson to run the Playgroup, and she and Mike share an interest in Country and Western music.

MIKE TUCKER rapidly emerged as a strong union man when he took over as dairy manager at Brookfield in 1973. He called a meeting of farmworkers to revive the local NUAAW branch, and the following year became its secretary. He also campaigned about 'farm safety' and gave lectures on first aid, but upset some villagers when he refused to join the Ambridge Chorale (despite having a fine singing voice) and walked out of the Harvest Supper when the vicar started to appeal for money. By 1977

he was helping with the Youth Club (he lit the Ambridge Jubilee Beacon on their behalf) and in 1978 he became a farmer in his own right when Haydn Evans offered to take him into partnership at Willow Farm. He and his wife Betty had to raise a substantial amount of money from the bank, and Dan Archer also lent them money to buy stock. To meet their bills Mike took on a milk round and Betty took in bed-and-breakfast guests. In 1982 Haydn Evans decided to sell Willow Farm and move back to Wales, and for a time it looked as if the Tuckers would be homeless and without a livelihood. In the event the tenancy of Ambridge Farm became available, and Mike was offered it by the Bellamy Estate.

MARTHA WOODFORD used to be Martha Lily, whose husband Herbert was the Penny Hassett postman. In 1961 Herbert died, and ten years later Martha came to work at the Field Centre in Ambridge and became friendly with Joe Grundy (she spent Christmas with him in 1971) and then even friendlier with Joby Woodford the woodman. She and Joby were married on Christmas Day, 1972, and at first Martha worked as a petrol pump attendant and cleaning lady, but eventually she was given the village shop to run.

Joby died in January 1983, and for a few months it seemed that Martha was trying to contact him through a spiritualist. In time, though, her attention was distracted by something more earthy: Joe Grundy (believing her to have a tidy nest-egg, and being very fond of her puddings) started to court her, reviving the friendship of their earlier days. Then Bill Insley, a retired farmer living at Willow Farm, also started to call and help her about the house.

Both Bill and Joe made bird tables for her, but the joy of having two male admirers did not last. When Joe invited her to see *Mary Poppins* at the Borchester Odeon she turned him down in favour of

Jethro Larkin advises retired Derbyshire farmer Bill Insley on the benefits and drawbacks of buying Willow Farm, 1983. Ted Moult (Bill Insley).

Bill Insley – who took her to look at a pig farm instead of to the seaside.

HAZEL WOOLLEY is the only daughter of Reggie and Valerie Trentham, and was born in 1956. She spent her early years in the West Indies, but when her father died her mother brought her back to Ambridge. Valerie's second marriage was to Jack Woolley, and although it did not last, Woolley went ahead with his plans to formally adopt Hazel as his daughter. When Valerie walked out Hazel stayed, was educated by Woolley, and given an allowance by him when she eventually moved to London.

She sometimes works as a PA in a film company, and to Woolley's disappointment hardly ever comes to visit him. When she does, though, she usually makes an impact. In 1983 she attempted (out of boredom) to seduce Tony Archer and then sacked Higgs; in 1984 she kicked Captain (Nigel Pargetter called her a 'she-wolf') and poured vodka in the fish tank (killing all the fishes). In August 1985, she again returned and Woolley gave her a post as conference manager and PRO.

In the elegant dining-room at Grey Gables, Jack Woolley and his restaurant manageress Caroline ponder over the claret.

JACK WOOLLEY came to Ambridge in 1962, when he bought Grey Gables Country Club from Reggie and Valerie Trentham and resolved to turn it into an 'exclusive holiday centre for tired business executives.' A self-made man from Stirchley, Birmingham, Jack had a sister, Marjorie, who is now dead. In 1966 Jack married Valerie Trentham (Reggie had died in the West Indies) and in 1969 he formally adopted Valerie's daughter Hazel. Soon after, Valerie walked out on him. In 1973 he was seriously injured after a robbery at Grey Gables and was unconscious for several days. He recovered to learn that Valerie was demanding a divorce, and soon after had a heart attack. He proposed marriage to Peggy Archer who turned him down. Overcoming these troubles he worked hard to build Grey Gables into a fine Country House Hotel and developed his business interests in the area – he owns the village shop and the *Borchester Echo*. In 1978 he bought the glebe fields south of the Am from the Church Commissioners and built a small, exclusive development of houses on them called 'Glebelands'. In March 1984 he was unconscious in hospital for several days yet again, after falling off the conservatory roof while trying to rescue his bull-terrier Captain. Later in the year, however, fortune smiled when he won the overall championship at the Borchester Chrysanthemum Show.

Above: Jovial Nigel Pargetter leads the way after a pleasant lunchtime in the cocktail bar with Caroline, Nelson, Jennifer, and Lizzie.

Below: A scene in The Bull, 1984.

Some Notable Archers Weddings

'Easter Monday,' said the BBC announcer one April evening in 1955, 'and in Ambridge a milestone for the Archers and the Fairbrothers, for today the families are to be united by the marriage of Phil and Grace....' It was also a milestone for the programme: the first in a long line of notable weddings to be heard on the air. Phil had wooed Grace for four tempestuous years before they finally reached the altar of St Stephen's, where Grace promised to love, honour, and obey him as long as they both should live – which was not, as we now know, going

September 1985, Shula and Mark's wedding. Bridesmaids Elizabeth Archer and Kate Aldridge reflect over a bowl of strawberries.

to be for very long. But no black clouds marred the happy day – except for Dan complaining bitterly to Doris: 'Do I have to put this weskit on?' Dan also had a drop of whisky with Phil before the event, and the sound-effect note on the script reads: TWO DRINKS POURED – VERY SHORT ONES ON POLICY GROUNDS which shows that the '*Why is there so much drinking in "The Archers"?*' lobby was as vociferous thirty years ago as it is today.

Dan and Phil had their small drinks, and Dan said: 'Don't want any advice from me do you?' and Phil said: 'I'm a big boy now, Dad,' and off they went to church. Brother Jack was an even bigger boy, but he didn't behave like one when he sneaked

The first Archers wedding to be heard – the marriage of Phil and Grace, recorded in Hanbury Church, March 1955.

The bride

The family group

Tony and Pat

(*Opposite above*) Elizabeth, David and Shula

(*Opposite below*) Walter, Tom and Jethro

The bridesmaids

off to sabotage the honeymoon car. 'Vaseline and confetti,' he chortled, 'kippers on the exhaust pipe, boots, and enamel bedroomware ...' As the couple finally swept off from the reception, scriptwriters Ted Mason and Geoffrey Webb recaptured the excitement of their old *Dick Barton* days, making Phil speed in and out of fields and woods to avoid pursuit by Valerie and Reggie Trentham, and Chris and Paul. 'It's a chase, wifie mine,' yelled an exuberant Phil. 'We'll give them a run for their money!'

A year or more passed; Grace died after the stables fire, Phil took up cine photography, and Christine Archer was proposed-to by dashing horse-owner Paul Johnson. They were married in December 1956. Christine wore a white lace dress with paper taffeta petticoats, and Doris wore an empire-line dress of purple silk. John Tregorran helped Phil to make a cine film of the event. Perhaps this was radio's answer to the growing threat of television – describing the pictures we so sadly lacked. 'Get a long shot at the church porch,' instructed John Tregorran, 'pan right round with them as they come through it, and have a close-up as they're getting into the car.' And Dan reminded us that Ambridge, too, was suffering from the Suez crisis: 'Wonder how these car hire firms'll do for petrol under the rationing scheme?'

Brother Jack, the fun-loving wedding fiend, was strangely quiet at his sister's wedding, but made up for it a year later when Phil married Jill Patterson, a girl he had espied through his cine camera (bright yellow dress and urchin haircut) at the Ambridge Fête. Once again Jack was creeping away from the reception and reporting back to Peggy: 'Confetti in every pocket! Twenty pin-ups of the Jane Mansfield variety tucked in Phil's case and a dozen-odd Rod Steigers, Marlon Brandos and the like in Jill's!' He gave Paul some kippers and sent him off to find the honeymoon car, and as the bride and groom left he started throwing things. 'Hey, come off it,' shouted Phil. 'The hotel specifically said no confetti.'

'They didn't say anything about rice, though,' yelled Jack. 'All right folks! Let 'em have it!'

The wedding had taken place quietly in Crudley

Church – the only occasion, as far as one can tell, that the programme has ever visited Crudley, home of the orphan Jill – and the only guests, apart from the immediate family, were Grace's parents, Helen and George Fairbrother, who gave the happy couple a second-hand 1952 motor car as a wedding present.

It was almost a decade before the Archer family were involved in another wedding, and it wasn't really an 'Archer' wedding at all. But when Sid Perks married Polly Mead it was fun-loving Jack Archer who gave the bride away (her father being locked securely in the county mental hospital after having been proved to be a keen arsonist) and for good measure Jennifer and Lilian were drafted in

The wedding of Sid and Polly Perks made headlines in the *Borchester Echo*.

When Lilian married Ralph Bellamy in September 1971,
Tony gave the bride away (Jack was ill in a sanatorium) and
Jennifer was matron of honour.

as bridesmaids and rigged out in ornate blue bro-
cade dresses. Jennifer, a 1960s-girl, exclaimed:
'Give me the jeans and the mini skirts every time!'
and then went on: 'What a fuss and palaver all for
the sake of bringing together a man and woman in
holy wedlock!' It was 27 September 1966, and Jack
found he was losing his taste for wedding mirth. 'I'll
be glad when it's all over,' he confessed, 'I haven't
been to the old casino for days.'

Sid and Polly were sent on honeymoon to Devon
(paid for by a munificent Jack Woolley) and the
Archer family had no wedding presents to buy for
two years. Then, Jennifer with her jeans and mini-
skirts and little illegitimate baby called Adam was
married at Borchester register office to smoothie
Roger Travers-Macy. They had a reception at the
Duke Hotel, Borchester (which hasn't been heard of
since), went for a weekend in London, came back to
collect Adam from Doris's motherly care, and flew

off to Ibiza for a holiday. The following year, 1969,
Lilian married airforce pilot Lester Nicholson, but
it was two years later, with poor Lester dead and
buried, that Lilian made her real catch – the Squire
of Ambridge himself, Ralph Bellamy.

The reception was at Grey Gables, and the
groom's gift to the bride was first a portrait of herself on *Red Knight* and then (as the guests peered,
as instructed, out of the windows) *Red Knight* itself.
It was a posh and proper wedding with one absent
guest – Jack, who was lying too weak to be moved
in a Scottish sanatorium. 'It won't seem the same
without him,' said Doris, thinking perhaps of the
rice and the kippers and pictures of Marlon Brando.
'No love,' said Dan. 'But don't mention it, will you?
Not to Peggy or Lilian or anyone ... because it's a
kind of grim game we're all playing.'

Pat and Tony were married at the end of 1974. In
St Stephen's the vicar said to Pat: 'Wilt thou have
this man to be thy wedded husband, to live together

Shula and Mark Hebden posing for a photograph at their
wedding reception.

Best man Nigel Pargetter and the groom.

A toast to the happy couple from Walter Gabriel.

after God's holy ordinance in the holy estate of matrimony? Wilt thou obey him and serve him, love, honour and keep him ...' and Pat said (firmly, according to the script), 'I will.' At the reception Peggy said 'Congratulations' and Tony said 'Thanks, Mum' and Pat said: 'I'll look after him, Mrs Archer.'

Thirty years on from his first marriage, Phil Archer saw his elder daughter Shula married to Mark Hebden in St Stephen's church – the first of a new generation to be married from Brookfield Farm; with Elizabeth, David, and (who knows?) Kenton to come.

The wedding took place in September, but the photographs were taken in April at Hagley Hall in Worcestershire, a stately home where Lord and Lady Cobham are used to hosting every sort of event from wedding receptions to horse trials. After considerable searching the most romantic wedding gown was found at Pronuptia (de Paris and Birmingham) and the air of opulence was aided by the magnificent whole dressed salmon at the centre of the wedding feast.

It was, though, like everything else on 'The Archers', just illusion. When it was over the wedding gown went back to Pronuptia, and the salmon back to the kitchen untouched. Only Patrick Lichfield was real.

Above: Nigel and Elizabeth.

Centre: Jethro Larkin and daughter Clarrie.

Right: Mrs Perkins and daughter Peggy.

THE CAST

BOB ARNOLD (Tom Forrest) was born on Boxing Day, 1910, in the Cotswold village of Asthall, which lies in the Windrush Valley half-way between Minster Lovell and Burford. He didn't make much progress at school (so he says) and when he was fourteen he started work for a butcher in Burford and was paid five shillings a week.

'My father kept the village pub at Asthall, known then as the "Three Horse Shoes", but sadly it didn't make enough profit to support us,' Bob says. More troubles came in 1932 when he was taken seriously ill and spent fifteen months in hospital with a tubercular spine. 'When I came out of hospital the only job I could get was painting white lines on roads for Oxfordshire County Council.'

It was during his youth, growing up in the village 'local', that Bob heard the old men singing traditional Cotswold folk songs, and years later he remembered the words and the music and put them on record.

In 1937 Bob got his big chance in broadcasting. A programme called 'In the Cotswolds' was being made, and as Bob was well-known round Burford as a young singer and 'teller of stories' he was invited to take part. That led to other BBC Midlands programmes, and he soon found himself being billed in variety shows as 'Bob Arnold – the Farmer's Boy!'

After the war, which he spent in the RAF, he started to get steady work on Children's Hour and in radio drama, and then, in 1950, he auditioned for 'The Archers' and was told: 'You'll never be used by us because you've such a recognizable accent.'

There was a change of heart, though, and some four months later he was offered the part of Tom Forrest. He's been playing it ever since, and for over thirty years he's been introducing the Sunday omnibus. 'Like Tom I'm getting on a bit these days,' says Bob, 'but I'm still happy playing the odd episode, and we both look forward to being around for a little while longer yet!'

HEATHER BARRETT (Dorothy Adamson) was so amazed when she first came to Pebble Mill to act in 'The Archers', to be working among voices that she'd 'grown up with from being a little girl' that she forgot her cue. Now she's married to Terry Molloy (Mike Tucker) she hears an 'Archers' voice at home as well!

Heather trained at the Northern School of Music and Drama in Manchester, and had her first acting job at Oldham Rep before moving on to Manchester's Library Theatre. She has toured with Brian Way's Theatre Centre Co. and done an enormous number of radio plays from the BBC in Manchester and Birmingham.

'As you may know life in this profession is not an unbroken line of work, work, work,' says Heather, 'and in "resting" phases I have filled in with lots of different things – mostly selling, you name it, I've sold it!'

Once, she says, she dressed up as a fat, fluffy, yellow chick in an Egg Marketing Campaign, and knocked on peoples' doors very early in the morning to ask what they'd been eating for breakfast.

She also works from time to time as a television researcher. She and Terry have two sons, Robert and Philip.

JUDY BENNETT (Shula Archer) was educated at a Liverpool convent grammar school, and made her first public performance when she was fourteen, playing St Bernadette at a festival in the Philharmonic Hall. After studying at the Guildhall School of Music and Drama she got her first job as an ASM and understudy in The Chinese Prime Minister at the Globe Theatre – only to be sacked for not having an Equity card. She did a walk-on part in 'Emergency Ward 10', got her union card, and returned to The Globe as ASM/understudy in The Cavern.

In 1966 she auditioned for BBC Schools Radio, and was given her first radio job by Richard

Above: Trevor Harrison with his new 'radio father', Ted Kelsey, at Pebble Mill.

Below: Alison Dowling with Norman Painting and Patricia Greene rehearsing a scene out of doors.

Wortley, playing a boy. More radio work rapidly followed, including parts in 'The Dales' and 'Waggoner's Walk'. In June 1971 she joined 'The Archers' to play Shula – and she specializes in children's voices to such an extent that she has also successfully played brother Kenton, sister Elizabeth, and Adam Travers-Macy!

Her voice is often heard (though not always recognized) on television, where she has brought to life characters in puppet series and cartoons like 'Rupert the Bear', 'Mumfie', 'Cloppa Castle', 'The Munch Bunch', and 'The Perishers' – and on radio she presented the pre-school radio programme 'Playtime' for nine years.

She has also taken lead roles in many radio plays, including Pip in *Great Expectations* and David in *David Copperfield*.

Judy is married to Charles Collingwood (who plays Brian Aldridge) and has three children, Toby, eighteen, Barnaby, sixteen, and Jane who is six.

TIMOTHY BENTINCK (David Archer) is one of the few members of the cast with any practical experience of agriculture, having been born on a sheep station in Tasmania ('My parents emigrated there but came home for some conversation'), and worked on farms for pocket-money all through his childhood. He recently took time off to help his father renovate and stock a smallholding in Devon, and he's delivered twin lambs in a snowstorm on New Year's Eve and hand-milked a cow every morning for a year. 'I find some of David Archer's sneering lines about organic farming stick in my throat,' he says, 'not to mention his mockery of long-haired Liberals who work in television – since that's precisely what I am!'

Born in 1953 Tim was educated at Harrow, the University of East Anglia, and the Bristol Old Vic Theatre School. His first film role was as Roger Moore's right-hand man in *North Sea Hijack* and he has also been seen in *Pirates of Penzance, Success is the best Revenge* and the Channel 4 film *Winter Flight*.

Theatre credits include the Edinburgh fringe, rep at Plymouth and Coventry, and the *Pirates of Penzance* at Drury Lane. 'The pinnacle of my theatrical career so far was when I played the Pirate King for three weeks between Tim Curry and Oliver Tobias.'

Tim Bentinck

On television Tim has paid his mortgage by being the Opal Fruits' scoutmaster and appearing 'guinless' but surrounded by beautiful girls, but he is best known for his role as Tom Lacey in the BBC serial 'By the Sword Divided'.

When not acting he writes and records music, and recently provided the theme tune and incidental music to Michael Abbensett's play *Easy Money*. He lives in a Victorian house in Islington which he is slowly renovating with his wife Judy and one-year-old son Will.

BALLARD BERKELEY (Colonel Danby) received his greatest promotion rather late in life, when he was elevated from being a major in 'Fawlty Towers' to being a colonel in 'The Archers'. His own wartime career, in fact, was spent with the Metropolitan Police!

He has had a dazzling career in films, starring with Anna Neagle in *The Chinese Bungalow* back in the 1930s, and still going strong today with *The Holdcroft Covenant* and *Vacation 11* released in 1985. Notable film appearances have included parts in *Night Callers*, *Operation Diplomat* and *In Which We Serve*.

In the 1930s he starred and featured in West End plays including *Heartbreak House* and *The Ghost Train*, and made a personal success as Larry in *Love on the Dole*.

He has been in hundreds of television productions from 'Swizzlewick' and 'United' to recent guest appearances in the BBC's 'To the Manor Born', 'Hi de Hi', and 'Are You Being Served?'

Ballard Berkeley

Margot Boyd

MARGOT BOYD (Marjorie Antrobus) had the rare distinction while studying at RADA of taking part in a play being produced by Bernard Shaw, *Heartbreak House*, and that was only the start of a glittering theatrical career that has included many major West End productions. 'I was particularly lucky to play opposite A. E. Matthews, my favourite actor in comedy, in *The Manor at Northstead*', she says. In 1953 she did a season at Stratford, and it was then that she did her first radio broadcast from the BBC's Birmingham studios. After that came the musicals *Divorce me, darling* and *Waiting in the Wings* by Noel Coward, the play she has enjoyed acting in most of all.

Television work has included 'Dixon of Dock Green' and in 1969 she was invited to join the BBC Drama Repertory Company.

'Since then radio has been my first love,' says Margot. It was while working on the rep in London that she was given a small one-off part in 'The Archers' – and made such a success of it that Marjorie Antrobus was written into the programme as a permanent character.

RICHARD CARRINGTON (The Rev Richard Adamson) was offered his part in 'The Archers' in 1973, and reluctantly turned it down. Producer Tony Shryane needed him in the studio at Pebble Mill on a Wednesday afternoon and again the following Monday. 'The trouble was that on the Saturday in between I was due to be married – in Pennsylvania!'

Airline timetables were hastily consulted, however, and it was found to be just possible to keep all three appointments – so a wedding in America was speedily followed by a honeymoon in Edgbaston.

His most vivid memory of life in Ambridge is of conducting Doris Archer's funeral – in a real church with a full congregation – just a week after the death of his own father. He also remembers marrying Christine and George Barford (in the studio this time) and watching Christine walk up the aisle with her wedding dress slung over the arm of a sound-effects man, who was rustling it skilfully for the microphone.

Richard Carrington

Nowadays Richard spends most of his time as a radio interviewer, travelling the world to meet writers and record conversations about their lives and work. Among those he has especially enjoyed meeting are Graham Greene, John Updike, Salman Rushdie, and Peter Ustinov. And he thinks he is extremely lucky that a lot of his work involves staying at home – with his American wife and their three sons – being paid to read books.

SCOTT CHERRY (Martin Lambert) won both national prizes for drama students – the William Poel Prize at the National, and the Carleton Hobbs Award from the BBC – while he was at the Bristol Old Vic Theatre School. That led to a contract with the drama repertory company, where he gained valuable experience in radio techniques. In the theatre Scott has worked at Bristol, Ipswich, Northampton, and Westcliffe, and has played parts varying from Beckett in *Murder in the Cathedral* to Chaucer in *The Canterbury Tales* and Wilfred Owen in *Not About Heroes*.

Scott has also written stage plays, and his first radio play *Anything for a Game* – was broadcast by the BBC in the summer of 1984.

CHARLES COLLINGWOOD (Brian Aldridge) – 'I was born in Canada in 1943. My father was looking for someone to fight. He failed and we came back to England in 1944 and have been here ever since.' The young Charles Collingwood grew up in the country near Andover and then went to Sherborne School, where he shocked his house master by saying he wanted to be a night club pianist.

He did go to RADA, however, and embarked on a career as an actor. 'It took me six years to earn enough to pay tax,' he recalls. 'I did various ghastly jobs like cleaning and delivering boxes of fruit and veg. round Marble Arch.'

By 1973 he had worked with various repertory companies and was playing in *The Other Half Loves* with Penelope Keith at Greenwich. 'Shortly after that I met actress Judy Bennett, who was playing Shula in "The Archers", and we recorded three children's puppet series together for ATV – "Mumfie", "Cloppa Castle", and "The Munch Bunch" – and after we'd recorded 150 shows together we realized we were meant for each other and got married.'

When he's not working he's a passionate club cricketer, mostly with the stage cricket club, and a very keen gardener. He and Judy live in London, and their daughter Jane was born in 1979, when Charles was playing in *Dirty Linen* at the Arts Theatre as well as 'The Archers' – which made it a very busy year!

SARA COWARD (Caroline Bone), despite playing super-Sloane Caroline, has no connection, to her knowledge, with any branch, major or minor, of the English aristocracy! She is, in fact, a grammar-school girl from South-east London who went on to Bristol University and managed to get an honours degree in Drama and English while acting non-stop for three years. After that, she returned to London to finish training at the Guildhall School, where she won the Carlton Hobbs award. That gave her an Equity card and a six-month contract with the BBC Drama Repertory Company.

She went on to work in television and a wide selection of provincial theatres before going into the West End for The Prospect Company in *A Month in the Country* ('Which was very good,' she says) and then at The Ambassadors Theatre in *Let The Good Stones Roll*, a musical about the lives and loves of The Rolling Stones ('Which was very, very bad!')

Sara has also co-written plays for the London Fringe, the latest of which was a study of prostitution through 2,000 years called *The Oldest Profession* which was seen at the Bath Festival and was re-commissioned by the Open University. She has the distinction of having a chapter to herself in Clive Swift's book *The Performing World of the Actor*.

JAN COX (Hazel Woolley) feels that 'Hazel is a wonderful part for any actress to play. You could call her the J.R. of Ambridge – mad, bad, and generally upsetting!'

Jan trained as an actress for four years, and her career has been extraordinarily varied – from singing and dancing in a cabaret trio to community and children's theatre, working in churches and old people's homes. In her spare time she enjoys dancing, keep fit, writing poetry, yoga, and reading autobiographies.

'I got a few jibes from my friends when I started playing Hazel Woolley,' she says. 'Remarks like

Jan Cox

"Don't ever take her to a French restaurant, she eats the *chef* instead of the food!" I enjoy playing the part, though, and I'm sure there's some good in her. The trouble is, I haven't found it yet!'

Jan has played the part of Susan in BBC television's 'Juliet Bravo' and has been touring with *Rules of the Game*.

PAMELA CRAIG (Betty Tucker) first appeared on the professional stage as Peter Pan at the Theatre Royal, Leicester, when she was fifteen. After that she went to the Birmingham Theatre School, where Alan Devereux was a fellow pupil. She has worked extensively in rep, and spent several years working in radio drama in Manchester and Leeds, doing plays by Alan Plater, Henry Livings, Trevor Griffiths, and Alan Ayckbourn – who was a radio producer himself at the time.

In the West End, Pamela was directed in Charles Wood's *Meals on Wheels* by John Osborne. Television appearances include episodes of 'Z Cars' and thirteen weeks in 'Coronation Street' as Jackie Marsh, a journalist who had an affair with Ken Barlow. Her most recent television appearance was in 'The Pickersgill Primitive' by Mike Stott.

In her private life Pamela is married to actor Terence Brook, who is still recognized (despite beard and spectacles) as the 'lonely man' of Strand cigarette adverts in the 1960s!

ANNE CULLEN (Carol Tregorran) studied at the Royal Academy of Music during the war and was later to become a sub-professor there under Rose Bruford, and to teach broadcasting techniques at the academy for fifteen years. She was an adjudicator for the Associated Board of the Royal Schools of Music, and has also been on the examining board for the LRAM diploma.

Her acting career began in 1945 when she won the Royal Academy's gold medal for acting, and was invited to join the BBC drama rep. After that came weekly rep in the theatre, and work in films and television, and an enormous variety of radio work, including two years with Radio Luxembourg in serials like 'Dan Dare'.

She joined 'The Archers' in 1954 to play cool young businesswoman Carol Grey whose long, fraught romance with John Tregorran was to be one of the programme's best-remembered stories. She maintained her interest in the theatre, though, and played several lead parts at the Theatre Royal, Margate, with actor Monte Crick – who was the second Dan Archer.

RICHARD DERRINGTON (Mark Hebden) went straight into repertory after drama school – Birmingham, then Scarborough (with the Alan Ayckbourn Company), Salisbury, Nairobi, St Andrews and Liverpool – then, in 1975, he joined the Royal Shakespeare Company for three years and went to New York with the RSC's *Henry IV* and *Henry V*. After that he joined the Old Vic Company for their world tour of *Hamlet*.

Richard has been seen on television in programmes ranging from 'The New Avengers' to 'Pericles' and on radio he has played a host of classic parts – Feste, Puck, Charles Egremont in Disraeli's 'Sybil' and Oswald in 'Ghosts'.

In 1984 he gave the first performance of his one man show 'Taylor's Tickler', and since then it has been seen in theatres, pubs, and halls throughout England, and in June 1984 he played it for a week at the National Theatre. It has been recorded as a 'Play of the Week' by the BBC World Service, and in 1985 Richard was invited to take the play on an extensive tour of the United States.

Richard is married to Louise, who teaches the deaf and physically handicapped, and they live in a renovated cottage (surrounded by ducks and chickens) deep in the Gloucestershire countryside.

ALAN DEVEREUX (Sid Perks) is a member of the only father/daughter partnership in the programme – his real-life daughter Tracy-Jane plays clever grammar-school girl Lucy Perks. Born in 1941, Alan went to school in Sutton Coldfield. When he was fourteen he started going to evening classes to study speech and drama, and a year later he went to the Birmingham Theatre School. BBC radio plays soon followed, and 'walk-on' parts in television, and he made his first professional stage appearance at Birmingham Rep in 1956. 'I spent five years in stage-management with Derek Salberg's repertory companies at the Alex in Birmingham and The Grand in Wolverhampton,' he recalls. 'Working as an ASM in weekly rep, and playing small parts, was a very thorough way to learn about the theatre.'

He has been playing the part of Sid Perks since 1962, and has also performed in over 100 radio plays, supplied 'voice-overs' to countless audio-visual films for industry, appeared in three television commercials, and voiced around 6,000 radio adverts.

He still lives in Sutton Coldfield, has been married now for nineteen years, and, as well as daughter Tracy-Jane, has an eleven-year-old son, Ross.

ALISON DOWLING (Elizabeth Archer) – 'I wouldn't be playing Elizabeth,' says Alison Dowling, 'if I'd managed to achieve my first ambition in life – ballet. The trouble was I didn't develop into a sylph-like swan, I developed hips instead! So with my promising career ruined, my aspirations shattered, I was forced into retirement – undiscovered – at the age of eleven!'

Acting soon followed, though, with a pantomime

audition in Shepherd's Bush leading to the offer of a place at the Barbara Speake Stage School, where she trained from 1972 to 1977. During this time she appeared in many BBC television plays including 'The Love School' and 'Grange Hill' and in 'Bless Me Father' and 'Quatermass' for Thames. She also worked for Ken Russell in two of his films – *Mahler* then *Tommy*. 'In *Tommy* I was young Tommy's voice and so far that's been my one and only disc.'

Since leaving theatre school Alison has been constantly busy in the theatre and in television – she played Jane Hardcastle in Yorkshire Television's 'Emmerdale Farm' – and in 1982 she went to America and toured with the Barn Theatre Company. She also works extensively in radio and television voice-overs, film dubbing, recording plays and stories, and foreign language tapes.

'Being an Archer doesn't bring instant success,' she says. 'While helping promote the programme at the Motor Show an elderly lady came up to me and as I began to sign my autograph she said: "Oh no, not you love, I want Eddie's!" Then, on seeing my dismayed expression, she added: "All right, I'll have yours too, Shula."'

PATRICIA GALLIMORE (Pat Archer) was a successful radio actress right from the start, winning the BBC's radio drama competition while still at drama school in Birmingham, and going straight off to a six-month contract on the BBC rep in London. After that she was in demand for a wide variety of radio plays and serials, including 'Wuthering Heights', 'The Forsyte Saga', and 'War and Peace'. She has read several serialized books on radio, worked in Schools Radio, and for several years she was a presenter of the much-lamented 'Listen With Mother'.

She returned to Warwickshire in 1973, and now lives in Henley-in-Arden with her solicitor husband, Charles, her son Tom, and daughter Harriet. Apart from radio work she does films and television commercials and has been seen in television dramas including the BBC serial 'Spy Ship'.

She is, though, particularly well experienced in radio serials, having had a part in 'The Dales' and spent three years playing the part of Barbara in 'Waggoner's Walk'. She joined the cast of 'The Archers' as Pat Lewis in 1974, and became Mrs Tony Archer the same year. 'I hope', she says, 'that Pat Archer will remain a good wife and mother, and that organic farming will prosper.'

CHRISS GITTINS (Walter Gabriel) was born in 1902, and spent his childhood summers before the First World War at a lonely cottage in the Shropshire countryside. 'I remember coming home tired and hungry from school, which was seven miles away, and having to draw water from a sixty-foot well. I was very small and I was terrified of letting the windlass handle slip.

'Then there were the wild nights when, with a hurricane lamp, I had to go out to the old two-seater privy at the top of the garden, scared to death of the noises of the night around me. Once a Jenny Wren was attracted by the light and flew in through the air vent, and finished up tangled in my curls.'

Chriss went to drama school in Wolverhampton, where he made an early stage appearance as an extra in *Julius Caesar* at the Grand Theatre. 'I was a soldier at the top of a flight of steps, and didn't realize the chap playing the Soothsayer was hiding behind me. When he leaped out shouting "Beware the Ides of March" I was so startled I tottered down the steps wildly clutching my banner. The audience was amused, but Julius Caesar wasn't.'

Chriss has been in numerous plays during fifty years of broadcasting, and he's been playing Walter Gabriel since 1953. 'The war years were probably the most varied,' he says, 'making documentaries about people from all walks of life.' He has been awarded an OBE and in 1984 was the subject of 'This Is Your Life' on Thames Television.

PATRICIA GREENE (Jill Archer) attended grammar school and studied at the Central School of Speech and Drama. She was one of the first actors to go to Eastern Europe after the war. 'There were newspaper headlines about it,' she recalls. '"Actress flies behind Iron Curtain to play Cow" and that sort of thing.' After that she did a series of jobs, from being a bus conductress and waitress to being a model and a cook – and all the time she worked whenever she could in the theatre. 'In Wales once I even blacked up and went on stage as a coal miner!'

At one point she considered joining the Rank Organization as a 'starlet', but in the end she didn't sign the contract. Instead she concentrated on the theatre: the fringe in London with George Devine, and then Oxford Rep.

Then, in 1956, came 'The Archers', and a new field of acting altogether. 'I was so ignorant of radio techniques', says Paddy, 'that when the script called for Jill to throw coffee over Phil I actually drenched poor Norman Painting in prop water.'

Married and living at Marlow, Patricia Greene has a son, Charles.

MOLLIE HARRIS (Martha Woodford) started her BBC career as a writer, jotting down the stories and yarns she heard during nine years working on farms in Oxfordshire during seedtime and harvest, and sending them to producer Paul Humphreys in

Mollie Harris

Birmingham. 'They were used on a programme called "In the Country" which was introduced by Phil Drabble,' she says. In time some of her writings were accepted on other programmes, like 'Regional Extra' and 'The Countryside in the Seasons'.

After that Mollie wrote her first book, the highly acclaimed autobiography of her childhood, *A Kind of Magic*, and she has been writing books ever since. The latest – and most successful – was *Cotswold Privies*, which came out last year.

'I took an audition for radio plays back in the 1960s,' she recalls, 'but it was only in 1970 that I was given the part of Martha in "The Archers".'

On one occasion, she remembers, she was talking to an Old Folks' club when an elderly man came up to her and offered marriage. 'All this gadding about has got to stop,' he said. 'I've a cottage of my own and £1,000 in the bank and I'll make an honest woman of you!'

'I had to explain to him,' says Mollie, 'that in real life I was happily married and had a son and two grandsons.'

TREVOR HARRISON (Eddie Grundy) is a Stourbridge lad, like Chriss Gittins. He went to the Birmingham Theatre School and then worked in rep in Birmingham and Coventry as well as doing a schools tour with 'Theatre in Education'. After that came television, with appearances in 'Get Some In', 'Hazel' and 'Stig of the Dump', and he has recently been spotted drinking and chatting-up girls in an advert for Harp lager. Children know him from 'Jackanory Playhouse' and 'The Basil Brush Show' and for his reading of stories on Radio 4's 'Listening Corner'.

It was his characterization of Eddie Grundy, though, that brought him dazzling fame, three record releases (the latest being 'Clarrie' on Foxy Records) and his very own fan club. It has also made him wary about coincidences.

'In one episode Eddie was kicked by a cow, and the night the episode was broadcast a herd of cows surrounded my car in a country lane and kicked it hard.

'On another occasion Eddie's van broke down in the programme, and the same day my own vehicle spluttered to a halt.

'The greatest coincidence, though, started at the

White Bear hotel in Shipston-on-Stour, where *Radio Times* took publicity pictures of Clarrie and Eddie's wedding reception, pretending it was "The Bull", Ambridge – where Clarrie was the barmaid.

'A year later I went back to the White Bear for a fan-club reunion, started chatting to the barmaid Julia Cook, and now I'm married to her!'

Trevor and Julia live in Leamington, when they are not travelling round the country so that Trevor can close things down. 'Other actors get asked to open things,' he says, puzzled, 'but I keep being asked to close things, like a store in Oxford Street and a festival in Salisbury. It's funny, that.'

GEORGE HART (Jethro Larkin) was a former artillery captain in the 8th Army and is the first member of 'The Archers' team to complete fifty years in radio drama (in February 1985). He also has another rare distinction: he's the only member of the cast to have been given the freedom of the City of London.

'I was born in 1911 on a farm at Broad Campden and educated at Campden Grammar School,' he recalls, 'then I was apprenticed to silversmithing with my father, and five years after that I was made a freeman of the Worshipful Company of Goldsmiths and given the freedom of the City of London.'

That was back in the early 1930s, when George also met the girl he was to marry, Stella, and started playing in local amateur dramatics. First he took on the role of 'the dashing hero bloke' in *Poor Old Sam*, then he played 'the romantic lover bloke' in *The Ghost Train*. In February 1935 he took part in a BBC drama called 'The Campden Wonder', which was broadcast live from a cellar in Chipping Campden, and told the story of a local rent-collector who reappeared in the village years after two men had been hanged for his murder.

'I was paid two pounds,' he says, 'and in those days a studio was a microphone hanging over a carpet, and some marks on the floor telling you where to stand.'

On one occasion, he remembers, the BBC visited Campden to do a live broadcast with some mummers, and one chap got a bit fed up about being left out of the interview and said: 'Shut the bloody rattle!' to another chap, then realized what he had done, and said, horrified, 'That's buggered it!' There were newspaper headlines the next day demanding to know 'who put the B in the BBC?'

George had joined the Territorial Army before the war, and in 1940 he was sent to OCTU and commissioned in the Royal Artillery. From there he was posted to North Africa, and in the odd moments when he wasn't actively engaged in fighting Rommel he started up a concert party and somehow got hold of an old piano.

'We carted that piano from North Africa to Italy, then to Yugoslavia and the islands off the coast there, then back to Italy, to France, to Belgium, Holland, and then into Germany – and when I was demobbed it was still being played there in some barracks.'

Back in Chipping Campden George couldn't settle again at being a silversmith. 'I'd been out in the open air for five years, either under canvas or under a hedge, and I sat down at the bench and thought: I can't stand this! I must get out in the fresh air!'

He became area representative for Massey-Ferguson, but he also kept up his work as an actor and entertainer and took part in various broadcasts for the BBC. Then 'The Archers' came along, and he played a village bobby and a cricket umpire, and eighteen years ago took on the part of Jethro Larkin and turned it into one of the best-loved characters in the programme.

Of 'The Archers' team George says: 'It's just like one big happy family, that's the great thing, that's what makes it go.'

BRIAN HEWLETT (Neil Carter) is a keen photographer and bird watcher and cares deeply about conservation of the countryside and the preservation of wildlife. He spends his holidays – when time and money allow – exploring in Peru, visiting game parks in Kenya, and observing the rare mountain gorillas in Rwanda, and he returns to delight his friends in the theatre and the Pebble Mill studios with showings of his remarkable photographs.

Brian trained at the Rose Bruford College in Kent, and his first professional job in the theatre was as a walk-on and understudy in *Lock Up Your Daughters* at London's Mermaid Theatre. After completing *Great Expectations* at the Mermaid – his

Brian Hewlett

performance was favourably noticed by Harold Hobson – he left to play the title part in a nation-wide tour of Brendan Behan's *The Hostage*.

'My first radio broadcast was in a play called *Frost* and I shared leading roles with Chriss Gittins,' he recalls. 'Little did I realize how much work I would be sharing with Chriss in the future!'

Brian has been in the BBC Drama Repertory Company three times, but has always accepted theatre work whenever he can. 'I've been the Dame several times in Christmas pantos, love taking part in musicals, and had a superbly enjoyable time at London's Cambridge Theatre playing Amos Hart in *Chicago*.'

He has also worked extensively in television – from 'Emergency Ward Ten' and 'Probation Officer' to the recent BBC production 'Trelawney of the Wells'. He joined 'The Archers' as Brookfield's new farming apprentice in 1973.

EDWARD KELSEY (Joe Grundy) trained at the Royal Academy of Music, after leaving the RAF in 1951 and graduated as a teacher of speech and

drama. He also won the Howard De Walden Gold Medal and was winner of the Carlton Hobbs radio award in its second year of existence. 'Since then radio has always been my first love,' he says, 'although I've been involved in most other branches of the acting profession.'

His first theatre work was in the tour of *Reluctant Heroes*, and that was followed by many years in rep, notably at Guildford. He has made many television appearances over the years, most recently as Inspector Buxton in 'Juliet Bravo' and Titus Price in 'Anna of the Five Towns'. As something quite different, he has also provided the voices of Baron Greenback and Col K in the cartoon series 'Dangermouse'!

Ted does a great deal of writing and presenting for Schools Radio, and has just finished the book and lyrics of a musical version of *A Midsummer Night's Dream*.

CHARLOTTE MARTIN (Susan Horobin) was born in Fontainebleau, near Paris, where her father was working at NATO headquarters, and grew up at the family home in Solihull. At the age of three she started at dancing school; when she was nine she took the lead in *Babooshka*, a Christmas play, and at secondary school she was found in every play that was staged. After school she successfully auditioned for a place at the Birmingham Theatre School. 'I remember the day I was accepted. I was so elated I ran skipping down the streets of Birmingham with an enormous smile on my face, grinning madly at everybody.'

After drama school Charlotte appeared at Birmingham Rep as the maid in *The Importance of Being Earnest* and shortly after that she auditioned for 'The Archers'.

'It's been my biggest break. I still can't get over the way listeners are involved in the programme – when Susan had her baby I received several "congratulations" cards!'

In her spare time Charlotte writes poetry, but so far, she says, she hasn't had the courage to try to get it published.

FIONA MATHIESON (Clarrie Grundy) has worked with most of the major provincial companies, since beginning her career at the Mermaid

Charlotte Martin

JACK MAY (Nelson Gabriel), says his education was 'excellent – somewhere between *Decline and Fall* by Evelyn Waugh and *Sorrell and Son* by Warwick Deeping'.

Born in Henley-on-Thames, he knew from the earliest age that he was destined for an extrovert career. 'Barrister, Archbishop, Prime Minister (Pity' about that – Mrs Thatcher could have been my Chancellor of the Exchequer) or THE THEATRE.'

He spent the War in India, came back and was a teacher for a year, then went to Merton College, Oxford. After that he got a job at the renowned Birmingham Rep and stayed there for four years – 'with the exception of Paul Scofield a longer stay than any other actor' – and was the first actor to play Henry, consecutively, in the three parts of Henry VI, which he did at the Old Vic in 1954.

Between 1955 and 1985 he has been employed, he says modestly, as 'a jobbing actor', a phrase that covers countless film roles, leading parts in the West End, twenty-five television serials, and hundreds of radio parts. He's been in both versions of *Goodbye Mr Chips* and is the only actor to have played both Julius Caesar and Octavius Caesar in a major production at the Old Vic.

Among what he calls the 'unusual or bizarre' parts he has taken on he lists a film called *Cat Girl*, which was later described by John Boulting as the worst film ever made, and the part of a Chilean torturer in a play by Brian Phelan for Amnesty International.

Theatre, in roles as varied as Sally Bowles in *Cabaret* and Dr Scott in *Whose Life is it Anyway?*. She has spent long seasons with The Crucible, Sheffield, and with Alan Ayckbourne's company in Scarborough, where she played the lead in *Travelling Hopefully* by Ken Whitmore, a performance she repeated on radio. In London she has been seen at theatres like The Half Moon and The King's Head, and played the blonde bombshell in *Andy Capp* at The Aldwych.

Her radio work has spanned everything from singing on 'Midweek' to reading Woman's Hour serials, and many radio plays. On television, plays include 'Relative Strangers', 'Big Deal', and 'It Takes a Worried Man', but she is perhaps best remembered as the dual-personality French girl Felice in 'The Agatha Christie Hour' play 'The Fourth Man' which she recorded for Thames.

She's a trained singer and dancer, has a strong musical bias, and at the moment is busy writing a musical.

FRANK MIDDLEMASS (Dan Archer) was born in 1919, in the north of England, into a totally un-theatrical family. 'Parental influence urged me towards respectability and the civil service,' he says, 'a dreadful fate from which I was delivered by the outbreak of war.' He was in the army for nine years. 'When I emerged in 1948 I hurled myself into the theatre with whoops of joy. My first job was with a repertory company in Penzance, and that led to work in reps all over England – very happy years!'

Frank made his London début in a play at the Garrick with Thora Hird, and began to make the occasional broadcast and television appearance. Then he joined the Old Vic and spent several years in London, Bristol, and on tour. His 'professional wanderings' have taken him all over North and South America, the Far East and most of Europe.

In recent years he has concentrated mainly on television, and has particularly enjoyed involvement in 'War and Peace', 'Crime and Punishment' and 'To Serve Them All My Days'.

'There's also been the occasional movie, Shakespeare for the BBC and at Stratford; and Shaw at the Haymarket with Rex Harrison. And, of course, there is Dan Archer. . . .'

TERRY MOLLOY (Mike Tucker) was at a Playgoers Party in Darlington when a genteel old lady approached him and asked tentatively if he really did play Mike Tucker – this was in the days when Mike Tucker was an aggressive union man, standing up for the rights of agricultural workers. When he replied 'yes' she immediately started to hurl abuse at him, demanding to know how he *dared* to be so awful to poor Phil Archer. Then she hit him.

'Nowadays,' says Terry, 'if people ask me if I'm Terry Molloy I answer "Er, maybe . . ."'

Terry is also Davros, creator of the Daleks, in BBC television's 'Doctor Who' – and in a recent poll was voted third most evil creature in the Universe. But he has also played the lovable Toad in *Toad of Toad Hall* at Birmingham Rep!

Terry has done an immense amount of theatre work, including tours with the Cambridge Theatre Company and the Prospect Theatre Company and a national tour of *Godspell*, and on television he has been seen in programmes varying from 'Angels' to 'Birds of Prey' and 'Artemis 81'. On radio he has been in over 200 plays, and was voted 'Best Actor' in the Society of Authors radio awards for his performance as Boko in Ron Hutchinson's 'Risky City'.

Terry is married to Heather Barrett, who plays Dorothy Adamson in the Archers, and they live in Birmingham.

TED MOULT (Bill Insley) was born in Derby in 1926 and is married with six children. He has been a farmer since he was twenty-three – a dairy farmer to start with, but nowadays mainly arable and fruit.

It isn't, though, for his raspberries and strawberries that 'Farmer Moult' is best known by the British public. In 1958 he was a contestant on 'Brain of Britain' and that led to regular appearances on 'What's My Line', 'Ask me Another', and a host of radio and television quiz programmes where his rich country voice, down-to-earth humour, and astonishingly wide general knowledge were appreciated.

In recent years he has taken part in programmes ranging from 'Call My Bluff' and 'The Generation Game' to 'The Kenny Everett Show' and 'Tiswas', and he has emerged as a character actor in series like 'All Creatures Great and Small', 'Target', and, of course, 'The Archers'.

'I auditioned first for Dan Archer,' says Ted, 'and all the newspapers came and asked me if I could really play a chap of eighty-six. I told them it would be no trouble at all – my wife thinks I'm eighty-six now!'

HEDLI NIKLAUS (Kathy Holland) studied drama at the University of California where a tutor made her stand in large, crowded halls declaiming her vowels – 'did you ever hear anything as pure as that?' – and where she learned the method school of acting by pretending to be a jelly and made jelly noises with the department's 'jelly congregation'.

Hedli Niklaus

Back in England she took a more conventional degree in drama at Manchester University and started her professional acting career with Brian Way's touring Company in schools all over England and Scotland. Since then she has been in rep in Birmingham, Coventry, and Worcester, as well as Torquay, where she met her husband, actor Leon Tanner. She has been in many radio and television plays and presented the Tyne-Tees series 'Look-Out'.

Kathy Holland is Hedli's third character in 'The Archers'. She entered the programme as Libby Jones, a milk recorder, then came back as the Home Farm au pair Eva Lenz. It was while she was playing Eva that she married her husband Leon for the second time – he was also in the programme playing village bobby PC Coverdale!

She and Leon live in a cottage in Stratford's Old Town, with their son Nick and daughter Kate.

NORMAN PAINTING (Phil Archer) had his first broadcast in 1945, and he was first heard as Phil Archer on 29 May 1950, when 'The Archers' was broadcast for a trial week in the BBC's Midland Region. He has played the part ever since, and is the only member of the cast to have been in the programme continuously throughout its thirty-five years.

Norman did not, however, set out in life to be an actor. He left school at fifteen and after three years as a student librarian worked his way through Birmingham University, graduating with first-class honours. He then did research at Christ Church, Oxford, and became a tutor in Anglo Saxon at Exeter College. During this time he was active in university drama, both as a director and performer, and in 1949 he joined the BBC as writer and producer.

Since then he has written literally hundreds of radio plays and documentaries, including nearly 1,200 Archers scripts under the pen-name Bruno Milna (for which he and Edward J. Mason received a Writer's Guild Award). He has also become a well-known television personality in the Midlands for his highly praised programmes about gardens, and a national radio personality with appearances on 'Midweek', 'Quote - Unquote', 'Stop the Week' and Radio 2's 'On the Air'.

In 1976 Norman was made an OBE for services to broadcasting, and the Royal Agricultural Society have made him their only life governor in recognition of his twenty-five years' service to agriculture in the United Kingdom. He lives in a south Warwickshire village and is a trustee of the Warwickshire and Coventry Historic Churches Trust, and a patron of the Tree Council.

On 'The Archers'' twenty-fifth anniversary, he wrote a highly successful book about the programme, *Forever Ambridge*, which was updated and republished for its thirtieth anniversary.

ARNOLD PETERS (Jack Woolley) began his broadcasting career with a 'Children's Hour' programme called 'Hastings of Bengal' in 1951, and has now clocked up over 3,000 radio programmes, 250 television appearances, and has been in several feature films. He started his acting career at the Royal Theatre, Northampton, after service in the RAF, and spent five years in weekly and fortnightly rep before starting to get work with the BBC. He was a member of the BBC drama company in Birmingham in the early 1950s, and in 1953 he joined 'The Archers' to play Len Thomas – and when Len was written out, he played the vicar, the Rev. David Latimer – and after the demise of the Rev. Latimer, he took a break from Ambridge until 1980, when he returned as Jack Woolley.

Arnold still lives in the East Midlands, where he has written and directed several pantomimes, and directed musicals including Gilbert and Sullivan. He is married with one daughter, Caroline, who teaches ballet at a London Stage School. His hobbies include painting, dancing, and music, and he plays as a member of a folk dance band.

ANGELA PIPER (Jennifer Aldridge) unwittingly upset a listener who wrote very severely about her to Brian Aldridge, Home Farm, Ambridge: 'I know you do not realise it, but your wife Jennifer is secretly visiting London to read letters on BBC television's "Points of View". You must stop this. She is taking work away from a qualified person, and cannot possibly need the money.'

Actress Angela Piper ('Who says I don't need the money!') must have upset the above correspondent even more if he saw her in Yorkshire Television's 'Life Begins at Forty' and 'Third Time Lucky' – not to mention several television commercials, lots of film voice-overs, and a recent stage appearance at the Belgrade Theatre, Coventry.

Angela trained for the stage at the Royal Academy of Music, where she won the broadcasting prize. After that came the theatre, working as an ASM and playing juvenile leads, more radio work, and eventually the part of rebellious young schoolgirl Jennifer Archer.

Apart from her acting, Angela also adjudicates at Music and Drama festivals, gives poetry readings, opens fêtes up and down the country, and with her television announcer husband, Peter, is bringing up three children in a country house where they are all surrounded by dogs, cats, chickens, ducks, geese, a rabbit and a guinea pig.

GRAHAM ROBERTS (George Barford) is the only member of the cast to have played lawn tennis in the Wimbledon Qualifying Rounds (he also represented his county and the British Universities). Graham played soccer and cricket long after leaving school, rowed in the Henley Royal Regatta, and to cap it all was treasurer of his local Pony Club!

The theatre finally commanded his interest and after training at the Bristol Old Vic Theatre School he went into rep and then spent two years as Artistic Director of the Garrick Playhouse, Altrincham.

Graham was in the world première of Eric Linklater's *Breakspear in Gascony* at the Edinburgh Festival, the Royal Performance of Goldoni's *Venetian Twins* at Liverpool, and toured Italy for the Old Vic with Ben Jonson's *The Alchemist*.

Feature films include *This Sporting Life*, *A Taste of Honey*, and *A Touch of Brass* and his many television parts include P.C Aitken in 'Z Cars'.

Moving to Scotland he spent seven years with Grampian Television as a presenter and writer and now that he lives in Yorkshire he works as a continuity announcer for Yorkshire Television.

Graham is married to soprano Yvonne Robert, and together they make several tours each year with a highly acclaimed programme of words and music.

LESLEY SAWEARD (Christine Archer) recalls how 'In 1953 I was working as a teacher when I met the late Denis Folwell, who played Jack Archer, and he remarked on how similar my voice was to that of Pamela Mant, the girl who was playing Christine

Archer. I had been trained as an actress, so I jokingly said: "If she leaves, let me know!" little realising how that chance remark was to change the whole course of my life.'

Pamela Mant did leave the programme shortly afterwards, and Lesley was called to Birmingham for an audition. She got the part, and the voice match with Pamela was so complete that hardly anyone noticed the change. 'I've been playing Christine ever since,' says Lesley, 'apart from the years when my two children were born.'

Lesley has made many public appearances as 'Chris' over the years, and particularly remembers being given a standing ovation by members of the Women's Institute at the Albert Hall; and being very moved when a blind man presented her with the first thing he had made since losing his sight.

Apart from 'The Archers' Lesley works on film commentaries, audio-visual presentations, and commercials for both radio and television.

GRAHAM SEED (Nigel Pargetter) was educated at Charterhouse, and trained as an actor at RADA. He had his professional début with Sir John Clement's Chichester Festival Company in 1972. From there he went on to play many varying roles at Farnham, Perth, Birmingham, and at the Library Theatre, Manchester. His first London appearance was in 1973 at the Bankside Globe, and he followed that with two classical seasons at Greenwich directed by Jonathan Miller. He has also appeared regularly at the Theatre Royal, Windsor.

Although now something of a famous figure for his creation of Hooray-Henry Nigel Pargetter, Graham has also scored a big personal success for the past three years as Mole in *Toad of Toad Hall* during the Christmas season in London.

He has been seen in over thirty television plays since 1974. They include notable roles in 'Edward VII', 'Bergerac', 'Who's Who', 'Brideshead Revisited', 'The Cleopatras', and more recently 'The Front Line'; and on radio, Graham has been in twelve plays and has read Mozart's letters in 'Traveller's Tales'.

He is married to Clare Colvin, an art historian, and his main hobbies are cricket and snooker.

PAULINE SEVILLE (Mrs Perkins) trained at RADA and her first job was with the Manchester

Repertory Company, where the leading man was Noel Johnson, the original Dick Barton. In 1943 she went into ENSA and toured all over Britain and later Germany. More repertory work followed at Leicester and Newcastle, and then with Hilton Edwards' Dublin Gate Theatre Company at the Vaudeville Theatre in London.

Radio work has included 'Children's Hour' plays and 'Guilty Party', which was written by Archers scriptwriters Edward J. Mason and Geoffrey Webb. The part of Mrs Perkins came Pauline's way after her BBC audition was heard by Godfrey Baseley.

Pauline has not only played Mrs Perkins from the earliest days of the programme, she has also taken the parts of Rita Flynne and a girl called Audrey, who used to clean for John Tregorran.

Married to a Leicester businessman she has two children, a son of twenty-five and a daughter of twenty-three.

COLIN SKIPP (Tony Archer) started writing scripts with actor Victor Maddern while working as an office boy with the Rank Organization and he determined to earn his living from the theatre. 'Then my country called me,' he says, 'and I spent two years as a private in the Pay Corps.' His National Service was not without distinction, however, because he was one of a dozen privates selected to form a new 'Electronic Accounting Development Unit' – in other words to test out a thing called a computer. Released by the Army, Colin won a scholarship to RADA and kept himself in food and clothes by washing dishes at the Lyon's Corner House at Oxford Circus. 'I became hooked on washing-up,' he recalls, 'starting with all those messy dishes and ending up with everything clean, neat, and tidy. A perfect performance every time!' Colin still does the washing-up at his home in St Annes-on-Sea.

After winning the RADA fencing prize and the BBC drama student prize he went into rep and it was while doing a summer season at Guernsey in 1968 that he met his wife-to-be actress Lisa Davies.

By then he was also appearing in television serials like 'United' and 'The Newcomers', had been in the West End revival of The Long and the Short and the Tall, and had been heard playing a schoolboy in a radio play.

'I was asked to audition for sixteen-year-old Tony Archer, and although I was nearly thirty at the time I got the part.'

The age gap, he says, has led to some amusing experiences. 'When I got married in 1970 one newspaper confused my age with that of Tony Archer and reported that Lisa was marrying an eighteen-year-old actor. All her friends thought she was cradle-snatching.'

JUNE SPENCER (Peggy Archer) was born in Nottingham where she played Mustardseed in A Midsummer-Night's Dream at a very early age, and then went on to study music, dancing, and acting. She became an after-dinner entertainer, writing her own comedy material; and then went into the theatre and did a stint of weekly, twice-nightly rep. 'I decided there must be an easier way of earning a living than that,' she says, 'so in 1945 I went into radio, where I've been happily employed ever since!'

In the past forty years she has played in every conceivable type of radio programme – 'Children's Hour' and pantomime, plays in obscure verse, 'Dick Barton' and 'Mrs Dale's Diary' – and she even played the Virgin Mary once.

June was a founder member of 'The Archers' cast, playing Dan and Doris's cockney ex-ATS daughter-in-law Peggy in the trial week broadcast in 1950, as well as in the first national episode on 1 January 1951, and she also doubled as the flighty Irish girl Rita Flynne.

In 1953 she took a break when she and her husband adopted two children, but she was back in Ambridge a year later playing Rita Flynn and other parts, and she resumed playing Peggy in 1962 when Thelma Rogers left the programme.

Two books of her comedy sketches and a one-act play have been published, and she has also written a series of three satirical feature programmes which were produced by the BBC, and a number of 'Odd Odes' for Cyril Fletcher.

When she isn't at Pebble Mill, June lives in a village in Surrey where she spends a lot of time gardening, doing crosswords, bird watching, and reading.

DAVID VANN (Detective Sergeant Dave Barry) was born on 12 January 1951 – just eleven days after

David Vann

Television viewers have seen him in 'The Professionals' and the play 'Easy Money' in the BBC Playhouse series, and he has played many varying roles in radio plays.

TRACY-JANE WHITE (Lucy Perks) is known to most people as T-J, and her father in real life, as well as in 'The Archers', is Alan Devereux! Now studying English and Drama at a college in Cheshire, Tracy-Jane has taken part in amateur dramatics at Sutton Coldfield and school productions of *The Mikado* and *Iolanthe*. She has also performed a comic sketch ('Written with great success,' she says, 'by a hidden talent – my dad!') in the Birmingham Youth Show at the Hippodrome Theatre.

Tracy-Jane is nineteen and has created the part of Lucy Perks during the last four years. She says she particularly enjoys visiting country shows and opening fêtes jointly with her father.

Tracy Jane White

'The Archers' – and he confesses that as a teenager he rapidly acquired a taste for drinking beer at the Old Bull inn at Inkberrow, the pub on which The Bull in Ambridge is said to have been based.

'Other contact with Ambridge remained purely that of a listener until 1981 when Sgt Barry arrived at Borchester nick', he says. In the meantime, David filled his time studying for an English degree at the University of East Anglia (where he spent most of his time with the Dramatic Society) followed by training at LAMDA and finally a career as a professional actor.

Stage appearances include roles as varied as a punk Ugly Sister in pantomime, Squire Blackheart in *The Thwarting of Baron Bolligrew*, and Mr Brown in *The Adventures of Paddington Bear*. He has spent a season with the Chichester Festival Theatre and played in two productions at the National Theatre.

Moir Leslie (Sophie Barlow) the newest member of the cast, lives on a houseboat on the Thames. In Autumn 1985 she was touring as Ariel in *The Tempest* with Anthony Quayle's Compass Theatre Company.

Haydn Jones, who died in November 1984 on his way to record in the studio. A superb actor, he brought the warmth and humour of his own personality to the character of Joe Grundy.